Emotional Intelligence And Love Mastery

(2 Manuscripts)

Using EQ And The Sacred Enneagram To Learn Your Personality Type, Understand Your Partner's Language, And Improve Your Marriage And Relationships

JAMIE BRYCE & STEVEN MILES

1

CONTENTS

Manuscript 1:

Manuscript 2:

Couples Guide

To

Emotional Intelligence

EQ Mastery For Better Conflict Resolution, Perfect Communication, And Increased Intimacy To Improve Your Relationship

JAMIE BRYCE

marriage has barely more than a 50 percent chance of lasting," but this reasoning is a bit backward.

Think of divorce statistics as a descriptive tool, rather than a predictive tool. The current data on divorces is presented as statistics to describe what divorces look like in the world as it is at the moment. Divorce statistics do not predict or otherwise control how many divorces must be happening at a given point in time.

What does this mean for you? It means the divorce statistics don't define you, you define the divorce statistics. They have no control over you, you're the one who has control over them, just like you have control over your life and marriage.

Whether your marriage succeeds or fails, it's because of the choices you and your partner make, and not because of any statistical averages, no matter how negative they may seem.

It's also important to remember that these divorce statistics are incredibly broad, lumping every single sociological group into one big, broad statistic. Inside that big statistic, there's actually a ton of variety among different sociological populations. For example, *Pew Research* reports that college-educated women married between 2006 and 2010 have a 78 percent chance of their marriage lasting at least 20 years.

> There is a multitude of other factors that can affect a group's divorce rate besides age, sex, and education level. Religion, career, location, really every social detail you can think of can affect the divorce rate of a social group one way or the other.
>
> So, because your personal sociological details can greatly affect your average likelihood of divorce, it doesn't make much sense to worry about the average national divorce rate, since it's very likely it doesn't apply to your personal social group.

Emotional Intelligence, And Why It's The Key To A Successful Relationship

The problem with so much relationship advice out there (we're looking at you, Buzzfeed), and the many things we do to try and fix our relationships, is that it addresses symptoms of a struggling relationship, but not the core problems that are actually causing those symptoms.

Think of it this way: When you take Tylenol for a headache, you're not actually curing the headache. You're taking a temporary painkiller that alleviates the bad feelings you're having for a while. Sometimes, the Tylenol numbs the pain long enough for a headache to pass on its own, so we say that it "works" as a medical solution to headaches. But, we'd never call Tylenol a "cure" for headaches, because we know it's not.

We've all experienced headaches that come back after Tylenol wears off, and we've all experienced pains that Tylenol doesn't relieve. And we're okay with that because that's what we expect from Tylenol. We know it's not something that cures headaches, it's something that makes the pain symptoms go away while a headache cures itself.

The problem is that a lot of us are treating our relationships like we treat our headaches—meaning we're applying temporary solutions to pain symptoms, rather than addressing the root causes of the pain.

A suffering relationship is not like a headache. You can't just apply a common quick fix that might take some of the pain away for a while, then hope what's really wrong will just work itself out in the meantime. But, so much of the relationship advice out there, and so much of what we do to try and fix our own relationships is just that: a quick, painkilling fix that does not address what's actually wrong. This is why so much of it fails.

Like trying to fix a headache, people tend to approach fixing their relationship problems in a top-down, solution-first way.

"We're fighting too much. I think we should talk more."

"I don't trust him/her. I'll just take a quick peek at their phone to see who they're texting to ease my peace my mind."

"I don't want to see my in-laws this weekend. I'll just tell a white lie about work to get out of it."

While any of these "solutions" might work short-term, they don't address the core reasons for the problems. Is not talking enough really why you're fighting all the time? Is the reason you don't trust your partner because you can't see what's happening on their phone? Is lying to get out of one visit with your in-laws really the solution you want?

To really solve any of these relationship problems, you need to address the cause of the problem and not the symptoms. Why are you fighting? Why don't you trust your partner? Why do you dread seeing your in-laws?

To answer those questions, and to find real, effective ways to improve your relationships, you need to understand emotional intelligence.

What Is Emotional Intelligence, And Why Is It Key For Helping Relationships Succeed?

"Happy Tears Vs. Sad Tears"

Emotional intelligence is how we describe a person's ability to see, define, and understand the emotions of themselves and others, and also how well they're able to take that emotional information and use it to guide their actions.

It's similar to other measures of intelligence that you may be familiar with, such as IQ (which is used to measure and describe intellectual abilities like memory and logic) or physical intelligence (which measures how much control, skill, and ability a person has with their body). Similarly, emotional intelligence is used as a kind of catch-all term to describe a person's mental abilities along a specific part of intelligence—in this case, emotions. Also, like those other measurements, emotional intelligence has a long history of psychological research and scientific backing (which will be explored in more depth in future chapters.)

Here's a simple example of emotional intelligence in use: You see a person crying. To judge why they're crying, you use your emotional intelligence.

- You see their crying is quiet and soft. They're sniffling, but not really sobbing.

- Their eyes are mostly open. They're standing, sort of hugging themselves.

- In between the quivering of their lips, you can see the person is smiling a bit. They're shaking their head in what looks like disbelief.

Judging by those three points, your emotional intelligence tells you that the person is likely crying out of happiness. You decide to approach the person and ask if they're okay because your emotional intelligence tells you that even though someone is crying out of happiness, they still might need consolation or help because they've become overwhelmed by their emotions.

So, we can see how emotional intelligence was used to help us interpret emotions (why this person is crying) and guide our behavior (determining that this person might need my help to calm down). But, like IQ, emotional intelligence is a term used to describe a range of abilities—and not everyone has the same range. Let's revisit our crying person example with someone who has much lower emotional intelligence.

Someone else sees our happy crying person. Instead of correctly interpreting why they're crying, our person with lower emotional intelligence assumes that they're sad. Because the crying is soft and small, the person decides to try and cheer them up with a joke. They yell, "Hey, who died?!" across the room. This confuses our crying person, who takes the joke to mean that no one wants to see them cry, so they get embarrassed and leave.

Mistaking happy tears for sad ones can be a small and simple mistake to make, but as we can see in the example above, can make a big difference in how an interpersonal interaction plays out.

This is why emotional intelligence is so important and essential for the foundation of successful relationships. Emotional intelligence is what allows us to correctly interpret the emotions not only of our partners but of ourselves as well. It's also what lets us use that emotional information to move past the symptoms of our relationship problems and address the real causes.

Emotional intelligence is important to the health, growth, and success of relationships because it offers a way to affect real change in them. By improving how you interpret and act on emotions, you'll be able to make real, lasting improvements in your current or future relationships. Here are just some of the areas emotional intelligence can help you improve your relationships:

- **Resolve Conflict Better:** Higher emotional intelligence will help you identify conflicts sooner and resolve them faster before they escalate into serious arguments. When serious arguments do happen, you'll be able to diffuse them better and steer the argument toward a more productive and positive conclusion.

- **Learn From Mistakes:** Not only will you learn how to better identify and understand the roots of your mistakes, you also learn to better see how your mistakes affect your partner, making it much easier for you to gain the understanding and motivation to avoid such mistakes in the future.

- **Managing Your Emotions:** High emotional intelligence will help you take control of your emotions, by improving your ability to take a step back, identify your feelings, and rationally address the issues causing your emotional discomfort.

- **Managing The Emotions Of Other People:** Similarly, emotional intelligence helps you identify and understand the emotions of other people, enabling you to better manage their emotions as well.

- **Earning And Receiving Trust**: Build a foundation of trust based on honesty, understanding, and empathy.

- **Better Communication:** Learn how to better say what you really mean, how to be a good listener, and really hear what your partner is saying. Get better at asking good questions or otherwise respond to what your partner's saying in a way that moves the conversation along in a positive and productive direction. Give and receive feedback in a way that's fair and palatable.

- **Negotiate Successfully:** Improve how you cooperate and compromise with your partner, learning how to better offer what they want to get what you need in return.

The list could go on and on. There are almost endless ways that a higher EQ can help you improve your relationship. The question is, how do you do improve it?

Emotional Intelligence And Relationships That Can't—Or Shouldn't—Be Saved

It's important to note, and for you to realize, that not every relationship can be improved or saved. Relationships take the participation, commitment, and emotional intelligence of both partners to work.

It doesn't even necessarily have to be an exact

50/50 split of work between both partners, but if one person is not contributing enough emotionally to the relationship, it will not last. No matter how great your level of emotional intelligence and your mastery of this book, there will be some relationships that you cannot—or should not—save.

When talking about the value of emotional intelligence and the strategies that can be applied to it, this book will advise with the goal to strengthen or improve relationships. In part, this is for simplicity's sake, and it's also because it's the point of the book.

It would be too complicated and confusing to go back and forth between detailing all the ways emotional intelligence can help you improve your relationships, and also the ways those same skills can help you identify and exit bad relationships. The book would become too long, disorganized, and diluted in its goal of helping you strengthen your relationship.

However, much of the information in this book—specifically the portions devoted to improving your self-awareness, self-regulation, social awareness, and social regulation—will also help you identify and exit bad relationships.

How (And Why) Emotional Intelligence Is Taught

Emotional intelligence can be taught because it has components of being a flexible mental characteristic. Flexible mental characteristics are traits or abilities that you can consciously improve or change, as opposed to rigid mental characteristics, which solidify in early childhood and don't change much after that. Some examples of flexible mental characteristics are:

- **Linguistic Ability:** Through study and practice, you can learn new languages or gain a deeper understanding of one you currently speak, increasing your ability to communicate and what would be considered your linguistic intelligence.

- **Logic And Reasoning:** Logic has a long history of formal study, in both philosophy and science. These materials can teach you techniques that improve your logical reasoning ability, such as how to spot classic logical fallacies and how to apply logic to problem-solving. By mastering this knowledge of logic, you'll improve your logical intelligence and reasoning ability.

- **Coordination And Reflex:** Your physical abilities are considered part of your intelligence too. By practicing a specific physical motion—swinging at a baseball, juggling, hitting a speed bag—you improve your hand-eye coordination and reflexes, or "physical intelligence."

Emotional intelligence is like these mental characteristics, in that with practice and study, you can improve. This book is your key to doing so.

How This Book Will Help You Achieve Higher, Everyday Emotional Intelligence

Whether it's linguistics ability or emotional intelligence, the keys to improving any flexible mental characteristic are study, understanding, and practice. This book will give you everything you need to understand every facet of your emotional intelligence—from how you think about yourself to how you emotionally relate to other people—and give you simple strategies, tools, and habits to make the improvements you need to have the relationships you want.

This book is dedicated to everyday improvements in your emotional intelligence, meaning we're not digging deep into the emotional weeds or providing technical background for graduate students. We're focused on giving you practical, actionable information that you can use to make changes to your everyday life. It's through this simple, practical information that you'll be able to make real, noticeable improvements in your relationships.

Excited? You should be! Just ahead, on the next few pages, are your keys to building a greater, more effective understanding of emotion, and using that understanding to improving your current and future relationships.

CHAPTER 2:

WHAT IS EMOTIONAL INTELLIGENCE, AND HOW CAN YOU USE IT TO IMPROVE YOUR RELATIONSHIPS?

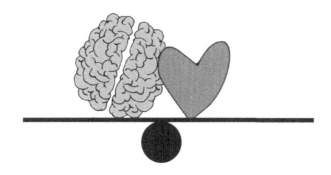

Before we dive into the strategies for improving your emotional intelligence, you should be made aware of some background information on emotional intelligence. While there's nothing especially technical in future chapters, some historical background, and context, as well as some terminology definitions, will help deepen your understanding of emotional intelligence as a whole, and also eliminate any possible areas for confusion.

A Short History Of Emotional Intelligence

The term and concept of emotional intelligence first started appearing as a modern psychological concept in the mid-1960s, appearing in psychotherapy journals such as *Practice of Child Psychology* and *Child Psychiatry*. While this makes emotional intelligence a much younger idea than other intelligence measures like IQ, which started appearing in the early 1900s, it still gives emotional intelligence almost 60 years of scientific development. So while it may seem like a new idea by some standards, it's been researched enough to become a solidified concept in psychology.

This is important to note because the terminology and tactics that you'll review later in the book are all backed by real scientific research and study. Emotional intelligence is not "pop psychology," nor is it an idea so new that the psychological science community is still debating its validity. (An example of the latter would be smartphone addiction and its effects on social behavior, something so new and complex that scientists are still trying to come to a consensus on the issue.)

What drove the initial definitions of emotional intelligence was a desire to define and describe aspects of intelligence that weren't covered by "traditional" intelligence measurements, such as IQ tests. By the 1960s, IQ tests were an established tool in the psychological community, and as a result of that establishment, scientists were starting to look at the information provided by those tests and wonder just how complete it really was. IQ tests measured mental abilities like reasoning and problem-solving in a very dry, academic way.

Could it be possible that problem-solving in relationships was an entirely different skill than solving an algebra problem?

Compounding this doubt in traditional intelligence testing was the rise of the study of personality in psychology. In psychology, personality is sort of the counterpart to intelligence—if intelligence is what you can do with your mind, personality is how your mind is.

Shyness, conscientiousness, agreeableness, these are all traits a person's mind can have. They don't really have anything to do with intelligence, and therefore would not be defined or studied by an IQ test, or any other measurement of intelligence. Instead, they describe elements of how a person is likely to act in a given situation. (How shyly will they approach meeting a new person? How likely are they to seek out new sensations or experiences? etc.)

The rise of personality psychology was important for the birth of emotional intelligence because it helped show that IQ and other traditional measures of intelligence were not a perfect system for describing someone's mental performance abilities. There were outside reasons for a person's success and/or failure at a task other than how smart they were. Maybe they were too shy to ask questions, maybe they were too extroverted and therefore too busy talking to new friends rather than paying attention to the directions for a task, etc.

Modern personality psychology began in the 1920s, with the publication of Carl Jung's *Psychological Types*, which laid out core personality psychology concepts such as introversion and extroversion. Jung, a student of Freud, is considered one of the founding fathers of modern psychology. His work in personality psychology created a lot of excitement and credibility behind the idea. By the 1950s, scientists had expanded on his ideas, creating the more familiar and complete personality theories such as Myers-Briggs Type and Type A and Type Personalities, which were conceived in the late 1940s and early 1950s.

It's in this crucible that the idea of emotional intelligence is born. By the 1960s, when the idea of emotional intelligence first starts appearing, psychologists are not only thinking about traditional intelligence testing and how it doesn't provide a complete explanation of behavior, they're also seeing personality theory develop and show a whole new spectrum for describing and defining a person's mental traits.

Unlike intelligence, which is considered to be a flexible mental trait, these emerging personality traits were considered rigid, meaning that someone's intelligence could increase or decrease for a variety of reasons, but personality would remain largely unchanging over the course of a person's life. A shy person may become less so over time, or learn ways to cope with and move past their shyness when necessary, but for the most part, a shy person will remain shy for their entire life.

While personality psychology provided a new way to describe and predict human behavior, it still wasn't what those looking for a way to describe emotional intelligence were looking for. The inflexibility of personality traits made them ill-suited for describing emotional intelligence. Because, while you could describe parts of someone's emotional intelligence as traits (how introspective they are, how much empathy they have), doing so doesn't really describe the action of emotional intelligence, which as we'll see in later chapters, is a crucial component of EI.

So, those who were studying emotional intelligence kept looking and working on their own ways to discuss, define and describe the concept in terms that made sense for it. By 1983, there was a legitimate breakthrough: *Frames of Mind: The Theory of Multiple Intelligences* was published by Howard Gardner.

Gardner, a prominent developmental psychologist at Harvard University, provided in the book several new descriptions for different kinds of intelligence that were not covered by traditional intelligence tests, such as musical-rhythmic and bodily-kinesthetic intelligence. These definitions represented the first real time that different kinds of intelligence were laid out as distinct identities.

And while it's true that emotional intelligence was not included as its own identity in Gardner's theory (it instead existed as a combination of several of his categories, including verbal-linguistic, interpersonal, and intrapersonal) his categorical requirements for different kinds of intelligence laid the key groundwork that would later be necessary for defining emotional intelligence.

To prove the existence of the new kinds of intelligence he was describing, Gardener created eight categorical requirements for his new intelligences:

- Can be isolated or destroyed by brain damage

- Has a place in evolutionary history

- Is present in the core operations of the mind

- Can be coded as a programmed task for a computer

- Has a clear developmental progression

- Prodigies and savants exist within the area, e.g., musical geniuses, natural athletes, etc.

- Empirical support from experimental psychology

- Empirical support from psychometric findings.

This was key to the development of the theory of emotional intelligence, especially because for the first time, some of the characteristics on his list defined intelligence as an action and as something that can be learned and improved upon.

After Gardener's multiple intelligences theory, the concept of emotional intelligence continued to gain momentum, appearing in more publications and journals as the years progressed. By 1989 or so, the term "emotional intelligence quotient" ("EQ") was seeing use in psychological journals. In 1995, emotional intelligence had its breakout year, when Daniel Goleman published *Emotional Intelligence—Why It Can Matter More Than IQ*.

The publication of the book is widely credited with popularizing and solidifying the foundation of emotional intelligence in modern psychological theory. Goleman, a longtime science journalist for *The New York Times*, combined much of the research of the time with new analysis to create one of the most popular and widely used theories of emotional intelligence.

The book is dense and full of valuable ideas for the understanding of emotional intelligence, but for the purposes of this book, there are three contributions from it that are absolutely vital for learning how to improve your own emotional intelligence:

1. **The Idea Of "Emotional Competencies" Which Are Emotional Skills That Are Not Innate, But Can Be Taught, Practiced, And Improved.** This is important because these emotional competencies get into the details of how emotional intelligence can actually be improved, and further establishing the ideas that emotional intelligence is not purely an innate trait that is gifted out at birth, with some people being born "emotionally intelligent," and others less so. It's something that can also be worked on and improved (to a degree) regardless of any EQ levels.

2. **The Idea That Emotional Intelligence Can (And Should) Be Both Measured As A Group Of Abilities And As A Group Of Traits.** Goleman's book sets emotional intelligence up as both an ability and a trait—meaning it's both a traditional form of

intelligence that is active and can grow and change, *and* a trait similar to a personality that different people may have different levels of. It may seem like a small distinction, but as we saw in our earlier discussion of the history of emotional intelligence, the point of flexibility vs. rigidity is an important one. By framing emotional intelligence as both a set of intellectual abilities and a set of personality traits, Goleman not only gave emotional intelligence a much more accurate definition, he provided it a much larger practical range for real-life applications, such as leadership training or relationship improvement.

For example, self-awareness is considered a key component of emotional intelligence. If you only classify self-awareness as an ability, you're defining it as something you do, like running or painting. And like running or painting, self-awareness can be something you can practice to get better at, or conversely, neglect and get worse at. While this is a valuable classification when thinking about improving self-awareness, it ignores a whole other component of self-awareness—some people seem to naturally have more of it than others.

It's important to also be able to think about self-awareness as a trait because it allows us to acknowledge that some people seem to innately have more than others. This is helpful when thinking about your own self-awareness, but the true value of this framing is in thinking about other people. As you work on your own emotional intelligence, you'll also grow to better see the emotional intelligence of other people, and see a range of abilities across many categories, including self-awareness.

3. **The Five Key Subcategories Of Emotional Intelligence.** Goleman described the five foundational subcategories as self-awareness, self-regulation, empathy, motivation and social skills. These subcategories are invaluable in thinking about and framing emotional intelligence because it breaks up the idea into procedural components. Meaning, the first step of higher emotional intelligence is getting better at analyzing and understanding your own behavior, i.e., becoming more self-aware.

Then, once you have this better sense of self-awareness, you can use it to move onto the next procedural step of higher emotional intelligence, self-regulation. These procedural steps are so important because they provide context and defined targets for improving your emotional intelligence. You're not just trying to become emotionally smarter, you're trying to become more self-aware, have more self-control, to understand others better, etc.

In our book, the last bullet is the most important. Defining the procedural subcategories of emotional intelligence makes it much easier to analyze and teach, and as we'll see in later chapters, also forms the backbone of this book.

Since Goleman's book was published, the study of emotional intelligence has boomed, resulting in a large field of devoted psychological study. There have been some changes and developments to the theory of emotional intelligence since then.

The most notable of which is that most emotional scientists have condensed Goleman's five categories into four*. It's these four subcategories of emotional intelligence that we will use to lay the groundwork for improving your emotional intelligence.

Each of the four subcategories will be better defined in its own chapter, but short definitions of each are as follows:

> **Self-Awareness:** Your ability to understand and "see" your emotions.

> **Self-Regulation:** Your ability to control your emotions and behaviors, both internally (how you feel) and externally (how you present your emotions to other people).

> **Social Awareness or Empathy:** Your ability to "put yourself in others' shoes" and understand the emotions, motivations, and perspectives of other people.

> **Social Regulation or Relationship Skills:** Your ability to successfully manage your relationships.

Today, emotional intelligence is studied and taught all over the world. It has become an important and thriving area of psychological research, and has also become an effective and valuable avenue for self-improvement. People work to improve their emotional intelligence for a whole host of reasons, from making their relationships better, to increasing performance in the office, to helping with raising a child, to just sleeping better at night.

Now that you've received a basic background in the history and definition of emotional intelligence, we'll move on to how it can actually be built.

---

*Motivation: The Emotional Intelligence Category Dropped From Goleman's Theory

The subcategory cut from Goleman's five subcategories of emotional intelligence is motivation. Defined as your drive to succeed, there is no doubt that motivation is at least partially an emotional trait. However, there are several reasons motivation is excluded from modern conversations about emotional intelligence.

- **It's not purely an emotional trait.** If you're hungry, it would be reasonable to say you're motivated to eat. If you're tired, it would be reasonable to say you're motivated to sleep. But being tired and hungry are physical demands, and you would classify the motivations that stem from them as physical as well. Similarly, you

---

may be motivated to make money, because you know you need it to live in society. This would be a conscious or practical demand, and motivations that stem from it would be considered practical as well. So, unlike the other four key traits, motivation does not exist purely in the realm of emotional intelligence.

- **It's difficult to define as a fundamental trait.** It can be argued that what we define as emotional motivation is really a combination of other more fundamental personality traits, like self-confidence (*I believe I can achieve things*), self-worth (*I deserve to have the things I need and want*) and imagination (*I can imagine things that I don't have, but want*). So, if you were trying to study or improve your motivation, you'd be better off studying these three components of motivation, rather than motivation alone. The other key components of emotional intelligence, such as self-awareness, are more fundamental traits, meaning that you can't really break them up into other, smaller traits.

- **It's encompassed by the other four subcategories.** Social regulation, social awareness, self-regulation, and self-awareness each contain elements of motivation. Self-awareness and self-regulation tell you why you want to do things, and how to control those feelings, while social awareness and social regulation allow you to do the same, but for others. So, in this way, the motivation category sort of repeats the information presented in the other four categories, without presenting any new perspective or ideas.

- **It's a trait worthy of scientific study, but not one that's very valuable when discussing self-improvement.** When we're talking about self-improvement, it's not very helpful to talk in-depth about motivation, as we will with the other traits. For one, if you're reading a book with the desire to improve yourself, you're probably already pretty motivated. Secondly, motivation is not especially teachable. While there are technically many exercises and strategies you can utilize to boost your self-confidence, energy levels, and self-esteem, doing those things requires motivation, so the whole exercise becomes somewhat silly, circular, and more about raising confidence and self-esteem, rather than motivation. Meaning, even if motivation has a place among the other four categories of EI, it wouldn't have much value to you personally.

Like what you see so far?

Please **leave a review on Amazon**

letting us know!

CHAPTER 3:

HOW TO BUILD EMOTIONAL INTELLIGENCE AND PUT WHAT YOU BUILD INTO PRACTICE

So now that you know what emotional intelligence is, it's time to get to the fun part— how we build it up and use it to improve your relationships. To build emotional intelligence, you need to learn how to identify areas where you can personally improve, then how to make those improvements. But first, let's talk a little about what you should expect your emotional intelligence improvements to actually look and feel like.

What Growth In Emotional Intelligence Does (And Does Not) Feel Like

In the previous chapters, we talked about how emotional intelligence is both a measure of ability(what you're able to do with your emotional intelligence), and a measure of a trait or how much emotional intelligence you innately have as a person. Abilities are flexible which we can practice and improve, and traits are rigid attributes that are fundamental to our personality. In improving emotional intelligence, you can always improve your emotional intelligence abilities but do not expect to change your emotional intelligence traits.

Think of it this way, if someone has a bad temper, there's a lot they can do to combat it. They can remove themselves from an environment that may make them frequently angry, they can take anger management courses, they can take up meditation, etc. But, even if this person makes great strides in reducing their anger problem, they will always carry that core of a bad temper in their personality.

The same can be said of the trait components of emotional intelligence. You may make massive improvements to your emotional intelligence abilities, but in spite of that, your emotional intelligence traits are unlikely to change.

You might feel like the person in the anger management example. On one hand, the person successfully managing their anger problems feels much better. They feel happier, calmer, and most importantly, a sense of control over their emotions and their behaviors. But on the other hand, they don't feel like an entirely new person either. They can still feel their anger lurking in them, and know they're going to have to work every day to keep making progress, because their inherent personality trait of having a bad temper has yet to go away, and may not ever.

So don't expect to work on your emotional intelligence to feel like a magic cure-all. You're not going to read this book, implement the strategies and tips inside it, and become a completely new person. Certainly, you'll make great improvements, and some of those improvements will be life-changing. But remember that some components of emotional intelligence are rigid traits, and even if you learn to control and work around them, they may never change, nor should you expect them to.

All of us are born and raised with all kinds of different personality traits, at all kinds of different levels. It's a fact of life, well established by personality and emotional intelligence research. The goal of this book is to teach you how to identify who you are emotionally—both from an ability and trait standpoint, and teach you how to work with who are so you can make the relationship improvements you want.

For example, a shy person may never be able to stop being shy, but they can take steps to combat their shyness and finally talk to someone they're captivated with. Further, they can keep beating their shyness and forge a real lasting relationship with that person. So while it's not really possible to change your emotional traits, you can absolutely learn how to work around them and create the life for yourself that you actually want.

Finding The Areas Where You Can Improve Your Emotional Intelligence

To locate the areas where you can improve your emotional intelligence, we're going to take a bottom-up approach. We're going to focus on understanding and improving the fundamental building blocks of emotional intelligence, then work our way up to addressing specific problems and/or areas where you can improve.

The reason for this bottom-up approach is that by focusing on the fundamentals, you'll be creating knowledge, tools, and strategies that can help you improve any and all areas of emotional intelligence you may want to, whether it's how to communicate better, how to trust your partner, or anything else you may want to improve in your relationships.

The alternative to this bottom-up approach is to look at your relationship problems from a top-down perspective, meaning you start with the problem and try and find a solution for it. This approach is inferior to the bottom-up strategy, because you may not be identifying your problem correctly, or seeing the whole picture.

For example, say you're having trouble communicating with your partner, so you start to search for communication advice in relationships. While you find an excessive amount of advice, your communication problem never resolves completely. This is because you may not have just a communication problem, you may have a communication, trust, self-awareness, and anger management problem. Because you approached solving your problems from top-down, you only identified the communication problem, but left the others unsolved—or they may even worsen.

A bottom-up strategy focuses on teaching the fundamentals of emotional intelligence. It avoids the aforementioned problem by giving you the ability to see the whole picture of your relationship—what the problems are, the strengths are, and what you can do to improve things by improving the foundations of both your emotional intelligence and your overall relationship.

The Four Components Of Emotional Intelligence And Why They Form The Foundation Of Improving Your Relationships

As mentioned in earlier chapters, the four components of emotional intelligence are:

> **Self-Awareness:** Your ability to understand and see your emotions.

> **Self-Regulation:** Your ability to control your emotions and behaviors, both internally (how you feel) and externally (how you present your emotions to other people).

> **Social Awareness:** Your ability to put yourself in others' shoes and understand the emotions, motivations, and perspectives of other people. This is commonly referred to as empathy.

> **Social Regulation:** Your ability to successfully manage your relationships.

These four key components encompass the entirety of emotional intelligence. Focusing on understanding and mastering these components will give you everything you need to improve your emotional intelligence comprehensively. Improving social awareness gives you the ability to truly understand your emotions, which is invaluable in relationships because it gives an understanding of your motivations and reactions to emotional information.

Once you understand those motivations and reactions, you can then use the next key component, self-regulation, to adapt, control, and guide those emotions in a way that's productive for your relationship goals. Social awareness and social regulation will allow you to do the same for your partner, so you'll better understand them. You'll gain the ability to understand their emotional reactions and motivations for behaviors, and also have the ability to manage and guide those emotions in a positive way for your relationship.

The next four chapters are going to discuss each of these four key components in much greater depth, giving you an understanding of each of the components and their role in relationships. The next chapters will also provide practical strategies you can implement to make improvements to your EI. Note, however, that these are not four separate skills that can be used individually. Each one of the skills is used in unison with the others.

Self-awareness has little value without self-regulation. What good is it to understand yourself, but not understand how to do anything with that understanding? Similarly, how can you self-regulate if you don't understand yourself well enough to know what you're actually regulating? How can you be socially aware if you're not able to understand yourself first? And if you're not able to understand yourself, how can you understand others, let alone learn to manage those relationships?

The four components of emotional intelligence are deeply connected. When reading through the next four chapters, keep that in mind and know that you're not building four different skills to help you improve your emotional intelligence and relationships, but one set of unified skills that will give you a powerful and versatile foundation to address whatever relationship issues you may be facing.

CHAPTER 4:

IMPROVING SELF-AWARENESS

Self-awareness is how well you're able to see your own feelings and understand why you're having them in a given situation. It's considered one half of personal competency, for example, how aware you are of your emotions, and based on that awareness, how well you're able to predict and manage your behavior. (The predicting and managing part of personal competency is called self-regulation, which will be discussed in the next chapter.)

We're starting with self-awareness because it's a fundamental part of EI. By raising your self-awareness to higher levels, you'll make the other emotional intelligence skills much easier to use. This is because a high self-awareness helps you make good choices, helps you identify and use your personal strengths, and keep your emotions from holding you back.

Let's spend a little more time on that last point.

What Does It Mean To Have Your "Emotions Hold You Back"?

We've all been there before—so angry, upset, or even excited that it's as if our emotions have taken over. It's an odd sensation, almost like your rational mind gave up control of yourself, and your emotions have overridden everything. It can feel like you're on autopilot, on cruise control, or like watching a movie of yourself or even dreaming. However you want to describe it, the result is the same—your rational mind is not in control of your actions, your emotions are.

When our emotions take over, that can be a dangerous moment in our relationships, because that's when we do things like:

- Say things we don't mean to achieve goals we don't really want.

- Say something cruel just to hurt our partner's feelings.

- Storm off, slam doors, or otherwise throw childish tantrums.

- Propose or agree to things that we don't really want concerning the status of our relationships ("I think we should take a break," "Let's get engaged," etc.)

Being taken over is referred to as emotional hijacking in most emotional intelligence research. That term describes best what it feels like—your emotions have stolen control over you, against your will, hijacking your thoughts and behavior.

Why self-awareness is so important, and why it's the first of the emotional intelligence components we're discussing, is because it's a key solution to emotional hijacking. By identifying when you're being emotionally hijacked, you'll then be able to use your self-regulation skills in the next chapter to break free from that hijacking and return to a more level and functional emotional state.

How does self-awareness combat emotional hijacking, and how can that help improve your relationship?

What Role Self-Awareness Plays In Relationships

Within the specific context of trying to improve your relationships, your self-awareness skills allow you to identify and understand your feelings on every aspect of the relationship, with a high degree of accuracy. With high self-awareness, your emotional interpretations won't stop at "He/she didn't call me back, so now I feel sad."

You'll be able to take it further and come to more insightful emotional conclusions, such as, "They didn't call me back. That makes me feel a little neglected and unimportant. Overall though, I've been feeling a lot of affection from them lately, so I guess I shouldn't let this one missed call bother me too much. It's probably nothing."

As shown in the example above, this improved awareness has great value on its own, by helping you to react better and more appropriately to emotional information. However, self-awareness is also a critical starting point for the three other key emotional intelligence skills. By improving your self-awareness, you will also gain the ability to control your emotions better, and also improve your ability to understand and cooperate with the emotions of your partner.

What A Person With High Self-Awareness Looks Like

To help you understand what self-awareness is and what it looks like in practice, let's take a look at a hypothetical person, and describe what she looks like to others.

How "Perceptive Paula," Who Has High Self-Awareness, Looks To Her Friends And Partner:

- **Paula is aware of how her tone of voice affects others.** Even when she's feeling angry or sad, Paula stays aware of those feelings and doesn't allow them to reflect in her tone of voice, because she knows that letting her emotions hijack how she sounds can make a conversation go in the wrong direction.

- **She is aware that she can be a pushover sometimes.** Paula knows herself well enough that she's aware she has a subconscious habit of being a bit of a people-pleaser at times—giving in to the demands of others despite wanting something different herself. Because of this awareness, she knows to look out for this people-pleasing behavior and corrects it when necessary.

- **She keeps her mind on the big picture.** Paula knows her long-term goals for her relationship with her partner. She uses this awareness to avoid making sacrifices that might go against those long-term goals, even though they might be beneficial in the short-term. (Examples of negative short-term goals would be agreeing with a partner just to end a fight, or choosing to remain silent and not speak up when she's upset.)

To provide a counter-example of someone with low self-awareness, let's look at another hypothetical person, "Short-Sighted Sally."

How Short-Sighted Sally, Who Has Low Self-Awareness, Looks To Her Friends And Partners:

- **She doesn't realize how her emotions make her seem to other people.** Sally is an excitable and nervous person, and she is not afraid to show it. She's often panicked at work, and worries over every little part of her personal relationships. She lets that worry show in her tone of voice and day-to-day behaviors and doesn't realize how that worry is making her partner feel nervous and defensive in response.

- **She has no idea how frantic she seems.** When Sally gets upset, she tends to spin out into a frantic fit. She has no idea this is an issue, however, instead, thinking she's successfully coping with an overwhelming amount of problems.

- **She blames others for her problems, instead of herself.** Sally has trouble distinguishing whose fault something is, often pushing off and blaming others for a problem, instead of seeing her part in an issue when something didn't go her way.

By looking at these examples of people with high and low self-awareness, we can see just what self-awareness looks like in practice. Sometimes, you can read the definitions of a term over and over, but not really understand it until you see an example for yourself, so hopefully the previous examples provided some additional clarity and understanding.

Strategies For Improving Your Self-Awareness

Here are some practical steps for improving your self-awareness. Remember, self-awareness is all about focusing on you, so get ready to tune in on your feelings and emotions. Don't feel bad or get frustrated if this intense level of introspection is challenging for you—or worse, it makes you anxious or uncomfortable. These kinds of feelings are natural when paying attention to yourself more.

Not everyone has the same natural level of comfort thinking about their own feelings, and that's okay. Maybe you were brought up in a household where thinking about or dwelling on your own feelings was not encouraged. Maybe you've never had a need to think about your feelings before—until you tried to really improve a long-term relationship that's important to you. If any of these situations describe your history of self-awareness, that's perfectly fine, and you have nothing to worry about.

Like physical exercise, improving your emotional intelligence is something almost anyone can do—some just have an ability to initially do so more than others. But also like exercise, the longer you stick with it, the better you'll be. Soon enough, you'll be a regular self-awareness power-lifter, impressing others with your ability to flex and understand exactly what you're feeling and why.

The strategies to follow are by no means the *only* ways you can improve your self-awareness. These strategies were selected because they're:

- **High-impact:** The strategies below are worth your time because they'll help you make big, positive changes in your self-awareness ability.

- **Foundational:** Mastering these specific self-awareness strategies is important because they're necessary skills for making improvements in other areas of emotional intelligence.

- **Distinct**: These strategies are different enough from each other. You get to think about and improve your self-awareness in different ways. It will give you more perspective on yourself, and also more versatile tools to get you there.

One last tip: Remember, these strategies are made to examine yourself, not make changes. Taking action and changing comes in the next chapter, on self-regulation. So don't worry that all you're doing is thinking about yourself—that's exactly what you should be doing at this point.

1. Stop Judging Your Feelings

From early on in our lives, we learn to attach a moral value or judgment to our feelings. "It's bad that I'm angry because angry people are bad people." "It's good that I'm happy because being happy is the point of life."

While there's nothing necessarily wrong with enjoying a good emotion (or feeling guilty about a bad one), placing judgments on our emotions can create an obstacle for our self-awareness. With emotions that are considered good, such as happiness or excitement, it's possible to indulge in them too much, neglecting to think about why you're feeling such positive emotions. The reverse is true for bad emotions. We tend to try and push them down and run from them because we feel guilty, bad, or ashamed for feeling them in the first place.

By removing the good and bad judgments from your emotions, you'll allow yourself to really sit, think about, and see the reasons why you're feeling the emotions you're experiencing. This is crucial for both improving your self-awareness and your relationships, for two reasons:

1. **By understanding the "why" of a feeling, you can make plans on how to practically address an issue.** Are you feeling happy that you got a raise because you're making more money, or are you happy that you got a raise because it means you're now making more money than your partner? These are two very different scenarios that have starkly different

implications about yourself and your relationship. Therefore, it's an important distinction to understand.

2. **Suspending judgment of your emotions allows them to run their course.** Worrying about whether you should or shouldn't be feeling something just adds more feelings on top of the emotion in question and prevents you from moving on and properly self-regulating your emotion.

   Example: If you're beating yourself up about feeling attracted to someone other than your partner, if also attaching judgment to that sentiment, you're adding guilt and shame on top of your current feeling and perpetuating the thoughts of attraction in your head. By suspending judgment, on the other hand, you allow the emotion to move into the self-regulation phase. You simply do nothing about the attraction, which helps your current relationship and allows you to move on with your day.

The next time you're reflecting on a feeling, avoid judging it. Instead, think about why you're feeling that way, and what it says about your current relationship or your current place in your life.

2. Pay Attention To Your Negative Emotions

It can be difficult to reflect upon and think about your negative emotions. After all, they're called negative for a reason. No one likes to feel jealousy, shame, anger and all the rest, but sometimes those emotions offer the key to the most rewarding personal improvements and personal growth.

The truth is that negative emotions often indicate a problem in our relationships or our lives. We like to avoid feeling them and thinking about them, because doing so causes us pain, but by doing that, we also cheat ourselves out of the opportunity to identify problems and find solutions.

Pay attention to your negative emotions and take them for what they are—an opportunity to make your life and your relationships better. It may be painful at first, but the more you do it, the more accustomed you'll become to moving past the pain and on to what you really want—a better relationship.

Practical Tip:

Try keeping a journal of your emotions. When first focusing on your self-awareness, whether it's on negative emotions or any kind, it can be helpful to keep a journal of your feelings. Writing things down can help you crystallize your ideas, and also take the sting out of negative emotions to make addressing them easier. Journaling is also a terrific memory tool, helping you become much more self-aware faster.

3. Don't Let Your Current Mood Control You

It's no secret that moods—good or bad—can cloud and control our emotions. When you're in a bad mood, everything seems rotten. Your partner doesn't understand you, you don't have fun anymore, and they're probably going to leave you soon for someone better. Similarly, when you're in a good mood: you and your partner are perfectly in sync, every second you spend together is a joy, and you're going to be together forever.

You can see that being steered by either good or bad moods can be problematic to true awareness of your emotions and the actual state of your relationship. To avoid being steered by your moods, try doing the following:

- Acknowledge that you're in a mood, that it's affecting how you see your relationship, and that it will eventually pass.

- Avoid making any big decisions while in a mood.

- Think about how you got in that mood in the first place.

4. Learn Your Triggers

Everyone has things they find especially upsetting, exciting, or even distracting. This category of stimuli is broadly defined as triggers, and these are things that set us off toward an emotional hijacking.

For you, maybe it's when your partner forgets to put away the dishes or has a loud phone conversation right next to you when you're trying to read, or when they talk over you in an argument. Whatever your triggers are, it's important to be aware of them, because being aware of them is what will allow you to control them and improve your behavior.

When learning and identifying your triggers, you must be as specific as possible. You need to identify the exact people and situations that are triggers for you because this will allow you to focus in on exactly what the issue is, which will allow you to maximize your self-awareness.

For example, say you absolutely despise your ex, Julie Jerkface. Every time you see her post on Facebook, you feel your blood boil in anger. It's not enough for you to say, "Wow, I really hate Julie. Every time I see her post, I'm overcome with rage." You should also think about what she's doing (posting on Facebook) and why it's so infuriating to you. (Perhaps, it's always pictures of her out to brunch with her friends, and when you were dating, you always wanted to go to brunch with her, but she always preferred to sleep in instead.)

By analyzing your triggers further, you can understand why certain situations are so upsetting. Taking the above example further, perhaps missing out on brunch was so upsetting to you not only because it was a source of conflict between you and Julie, but also because you grew up in a big family, and were often left out of lunch and dinner plans with your older siblings, which is something that's always bothered you since.

5. Connect With Your Physical Side

Steps one through four focus on building up self-awareness by identifying and intellectualizing your emotions, but there's another way to feel them—literally. Sometimes, the best way to get in touch with your feelings is to, well, feel them.

Emotions are paired with physical sensations. (That's why they're called feelings after all.) The next time you're feeling a strong emotion—be it happiness, anger, sadness, or anything else—try and focus on the physical sensation of the emotion. Is your body tingling in anger? Are your palms sweating with nervousness? Are your legs shaking with nervousness?

By focusing on your physical reactions, you're improving your ability to connect an emotion with a clear clue that defines the feeling. This physical clues often pop up before mental realizations do, so being connected with the physical side of your emotions can be a great way to give yourself a self-awareness edge.

Improving your self-awareness is your first step toward taking your emotional intelligence and relationships to the next level. By learning how to better identify your emotions and their causes, you give yourself more opportunity to control and guide your actions, through a process referred to as "self-regulation." You also lay the foundation for other emotional skills, such as social awareness, and social regulation, which will be discussed later.

CHAPTER 5:

BETTER SELF-REGULATING

Now that we've talked about self-awareness, it's time to talk about the other part of personal competency: self-regulation. Self-regulation is your ability to take the emotional information you get from self-awareness and put it into practice, using it to steer your emotions and behavior in the direction you want to. It's the performance part of personal competency and is what actually lets you break out of emotional hijacking and regain control of your actions.

It's important to note though, that self-regulation is more than breaking out of an emotional hijacking. It also has a long-term role in emotional intelligence and healthy relationships. Besides helping you do things like control your tone of voice in an argument, self-regulation also helps you stay on track with long-term goals and avoid short-term behaviors that could damage or derail those goals. An example of short-term behaviors that self-regulation can help you avoid would be selfish actions like frivolous spending, lashing out over trivial problems, and even cheating.

So, self-regulation is important to improving relationships in two key areas: It's how we break out of emotional hijacking, and it's also how we avoid smaller damaging or destructive behaviors and stay on track for long-term relationship goals. The latter point is important and is often where you'll see the best results in your relationships.

What A Person With High Self-Regulation Looks Like

Like we did with self-awareness, let's look at some examples of hypothetical people with high and low self-regulation.

Let's start with "Calm Chris," who has high self-regulation:

- **In an argument, Calm Chris always appears to be patient.** Even in the most heated fights, Chris is able to keep his emotions in check and communicate in a calm, patient way.

- **Chris does not let emotions rule his behavior.** Whether he's sad, angry, or even excited, Chris does not let his emotions guide the way that he acts. He stays focused on his long-term personal and relationship goals and acts in a way that would benefit them, regardless of his current feelings.

- **Chris controls his impulses for sarcasm.** Chris has a dry sense of humor and likes to tease people in a way that sometimes comes off as too sarcastic or rude. But, he knows this behavior can not only be hurtful, but put his relationships at risk, so he resists the temptation to make these jokes and rarely lets any slip.

Now, let's look at a counter-example of someone with low self-regulation, "Impulsive Ivan."

What low self-regulation looks like, with Impulsive Ivan:

- **Ivan lets his emotions rule in an argument.** Any which way an argument is going, that's how Ivan will be. If he's mad, he's yelling. If he's sad, he's crying. He lets his emotions completely dictate his behavior in a fight, often to disastrous results.

- **How Ivan feels dictates what he does.** If Ivan is feeling sad, he'll push loved ones away. If he's happy or lonely, he'll try to draw his partner closer. There's no reasoning for his actions beyond how he feels. No plan, no thought, just the feelings of the moment guiding his behavior, which often leaves his partner feeling confused and frustrated.

- **Impulsive Ivan is, well, impulsive.** Ivan has a lot of trouble in managing his short-term wants versus his long-term goals. He often spends more money than he should, just to get something he wants right now. He makes, then cancels or changes plans on a whim. He flirts with ex-lovers and colleagues without any regard for long-term consequences to his current relationship.

Strategies For Improving Your Self-Regulation:

Here are some practical steps for improving your self-regulation, allowing you to utilize the knowledge you've gained from your improved self-awareness. These are the strategies that let you put all the brand-new self-awareness you've built into action, which means you want to make sure that you have a decent handle on your self-awareness before diving into this section and trying to apply these strategies into your relationships in real life. Otherwise, you may be trying to apply solutions to problems that don't actually exist—which is never where you want to be.

That said, the strategies in this section were picked not only because they're high-impact, foundational and distinct from each other, but also because they work in a complementary way to the self-awareness strategies given in Chapter Four. (This is also probably a good point to mention that the strategies below are of course not the only ways you can learn to self-regulate. There are many, many more out there. The five below were picked because they provide you with the best possible foundation for improving your self-regulation skills.)

By working in a complimentary way, we mean that the better you get at one of the skills, the better you'll get at the other skill. For example, take the first self-regulation skill below: Diffuse negative emotions and impulsiveness by adding time. Certainly, to realize that you're having negative emotions or being impulsive, you need sufficient self-awareness skills.

However, learning to control your negative emotions and impulses will also help you recognize them more. Think of it this way: The first time you use one of these strategies to break out of an emotional hijacking, won't that feel good? And because it feels good, won't you be more likely to realize your negative feelings in the future, and use the same strategy to break out again?

Like with self-awareness, don't worry if self-regulation doesn't come easily to you at first. Remember that everyone has different innate levels of all the components of emotional intelligence, and self-regulation is no exception to that. This book—and improving your relationships—are not about where your abilities are right now. It's about how we can take them forward. So take a deep breath, relax, and get ready to improve your self-regulation ability, one step at a time.

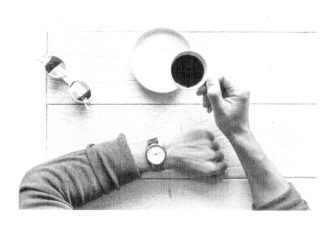

1. Diffuse Negative Emotions And Impulsiveness By Adding Time

Whether you're gripped in an especially intense emotional hijacking, or just considering doing something you might regret, time can be the solution.

If you're trapped in an intense emotional hijacking, try counting to ten. It may seem silly or absurd, but there's an effective truth in the old method of counting to calm down. By forcing your brain to shift gears into something else, you'll force your mind to switch and focus on a different kind of task—one that's much more rational and disconnected from whatever you're feeling. You may not make it all the way to ten, but shifting your attention to such a different task kind of has the effect of splashing your face with cold water—it's a soft reset and frees you from whatever you're feeling at the moment.

Counting to ten isn't the only way time can work in your favor and help you control your emotions. If you're struggling with a difficult emotional choice, whether it's an impulsive decision you know you shouldn't do, or simply a difficult emotional choice that you're having trouble wrapping your head around, often times the best way to ensure you make the right choice is to sleep on it.

Sometimes, a particular emotional situation or relationship is so frustrating or painful, our first impulse is to make a decision immediately, just to alleviate the pain. But doing so often means letting our emotions make the choice, not our minds, which can lead to decisions we regret down the road.

Instead, it can often be better to let your emotions settle and reset after a night's sleep. Usually, six-to-eight hours of sleep is enough to repress any reckless impulses or to allow enough time to pass to allow your rational mind to catch up with your emotional desires.

Practical Tip: How To Sleep Better

Sometimes when we're emotionally hijacked, sleeping on a decision is easier said than done. Your mind is racing, you can't get comfortable, and you're waking up every couple hours with the same worries or unwelcome thoughts, over and over. Thankfully, there are lots of things you can do to improve your nightly rest, from daily exercise to the overall improvements to emotional intelligence you'll gain from this book. Here are a few quick and easy things you can do to set yourself up to sleep better:

- **Avoid caffeine in the afternoon and evening.** Caffeine stays active in your body for an extremely long time, taking approximately 12 hours to fully pass from your body. This means that even a post-lunch cup of Joe can have an effect on your ability to sleep. A recent article in *Psychology Today* stated that caffeine consumed 6 hours before sleeping will reduce your overall sleep time by 1 hour, as well as significantly increasing the amount of time spent awake during the night. So if you want to sleep better, cutting back on the coffee is key.

- **Get outside for at least 20 minutes in the morning.** Morning sunlight is important for calibrating your internal clock and therefore putting yourself on a regular sleep schedule, so do what you can to get outside for a bit in the morning. It doesn't have to be sunny, and it doesn't have to be 20 continuous minutes, but it can't be filtered through windows or glass. So whether it's rolling down your car windows, waiting in the open air on the train platform, or taking your dog for a short walk in the morning, do what you can to spend a little time outside in the a.m.

- **Stay away from electronic screens for about two hours before going to sleep.** Similar to how the morning sun calibrates your internal clock for sleep, electronic screens can have the opposite effect. Bright screens like your TV, computer, and smartphone can make your body think it's a different time of day than it actually is, which can prolong your wakefulness and keep you from settling into an easy sleep. If you're someone who likes to browse their phone at night, note that while features like night mode that are designed to reduce the

> light output of your phone do in fact make
> it less bright, there are no scientific studies
> as of yet that verify if they actually reduce
> the harm done to your sleep or not.

2. Control How You Talk To Yourself

Regulating your self-talk, i.e., getting the voice inside your head to talk to you in the right way, is a critical component of your self-regulation. Research suggests that you have tens of thousands of thoughts every day, many of which are spoken to you by your internal voice. Sometimes, that voice does not talk to us in a way that's beneficial to regulating our emotions.

"Why did I do that? I'm so stupid."

"I can't believe I said that. I'm such a loser."

"He's going to leave me because I'm so ugly and boring."

Most of us have had thoughts like these at one point or another, and most of us know how such thoughts can send us into a miserable emotional hijacking, where we just beat ourselves up over and over and over.

Even negative self-talk like the examples above doesn't have to be so brutal. With some slight changes in phrasing, it's possible to smooth over and diminish your negative self-talk, so it's more emotionally manageable. Here are a couple examples of ways to smooth over the most common negative self-talk problems:

- **Instead of "I always" or "I never," say "This time."** While you don't want to ignore any habitual problems you may have, it's important to give yourself a chance to change and acknowledge each success or failure as its own distinct event.

- **Judge the event, not yourself.** We grow up learning to connect success or failures to ourselves, e.g., "I'm a winner because I did this thing right," or "I'm a loser because I did this thing wrong." But, not only is that faulty reasoning (winners also do things wrong sometimes, losers also do things right sometimes), it's misleading because actions are what can be right or wrong, not people. So, when criticizing your past behavior, it's much more accurate and helpful emotionally to say "I made a mistake when I did this," as opposed to "I was an idiot when I did this."

- **Avoid responsibility extremes.** It's important to take responsibility for your feelings and actions, and it's also important to blame others when blame is due, but rarely is it correct to say something is *all* your fault or *all* their fault. Doing so can lead to some particularly frustrating and inaccurate self-talk.

3. Create More Emotional Control By Harnessing The Power Of Positivity

One of the bigger obstacles to effective emotional control is being emotionally hijacked by negative emotions. Negative emotions reduce your motivation to do anything, as well as your belief in your ability to achieve your goals. Think of it this way: You may be able to picture someone who's too caught up in their happiness, but you'd never imagine that person sitting in bed, too afraid and beaten-down to make changes in their lives.

Breaking out of negative emotional hijacking is not always easy, but there are some tricks you can use and habits you can implement to loosen its grip and introduce some positivity into your life:

- **Force a smile.** This one may seem silly, but forcing a smile is scientifically proven to improve your mood. Research shows that even doing things similar to smiling, like holding a pencil in your mouth, is adequate. The smile muscles in your face are closely connected to your emotions of happiness so anything you can do to use them (even if it's holding a pencil in your mouth) can help you improve your mood.

- **Picture yourself succeeding at difficult tasks.** This is old advice, but there's scientific support for its value. MRI scans of people actually watching the sunset versus those just picturing it in their mind are virtually identical, meaning your brain has trouble telling the difference between what you're really seeing and what you're imagining.

  The value here is that you can picture yourself completing a difficult task, like having a hard conversation with a partner, as a way of practicing it in your head. If you picture yourself handling the conversation in a calm, positive way, it will help you do so in real life as well.

- **Focus on the immediate tasks at hand.** Sometimes being more positive can seem like a big, overwhelming project, where you're not sure how to start. When this is the case, don't worry about the big picture, focus on the next immediate step, whether that's getting out of bed to exercise, taking some time to write a short gratitude list of things you're thankful for, or even spending some time with some friends. By focusing on the immediate task, you'll find that your mind and body line and up and start focusing on the positive direction you want.

4. Get An Outside Perspective From Someone Else.

We like to think we have all the answers and can solve all our problems on our own—self-sufficiency is an important component of self-confidence after all. But the reality is, especially when we're emotionally hijacked, we can't see all the parts of our problems.

Talking about relationship problems with someone else can seem difficult or embarrassing at first, but it's also one of the most effective ways to break out of an emotional hijacking. By communicating you can get a new perspective and learn how to better regulate your current and future emotions.

We can get so tied up in our own emotions and our own needs, it can be difficult to see our partner's perspective. Talking to someone else who can give you an honest, unbiased, and outside perspective can be a valuable way to escape the emotional tangle of your own needs and desire to defend your side of the story.

When looking for someone to talk to, it's important that you choose someone who is not just going to take your side and tell you what you want to hear. People like your drinking buddy who's always hated your partner, your Mom who believes you can do no wrong, or a coworker you suspect might have a crush on you, are all bad choices.

Choose someone you can trust, someone you're comfortable with, but also someone who's going to be neutral and tell you the truth. Your friend who's known for telling harsh truths, your dad who's never coddled and always pushed you to be better, or ideally, a therapist who's paid to give you honest perspective and feedback are all better options. These are the people you want to bounce your relationship problems off of because they're the ones that are going to give you the truth and perspective you need.

5. Learn To Accept—And Expect—Change

Change can be intimidating, especially when it comes to our relationships. But, to successfully emotionally self-regulate, it's necessary to accept that change is a part of life, and will sometimes come to your relationships even if you don't want it to. To truly regulate your emotions, you need to accept that things can change, because you need to mentally prepare for those changes and think through the emotions and consequences that are going to come from that change. This preparation helps prevent you from getting emotionally hijacked by negative feelings like shame, disappointment, and shock that can pop up and surprise you when a relationship is going through a negative change.

Practical Tip: Write Out A "Coming Changes" Outline

To help yourself prepare for relationship changes that may be on the way, don't just run through them in your head over and over at night. Take your thoughts and planning deeper, and take the time to outline the changes you think might be on the way, and what the consequences of them might be. Then, write out possible solutions for those consequences. Even if these changes never happen, you'll feel better and more in control of your emotions from this preparation exercise.

Improving your self-regulation is a vital part of using your improved self-awareness and higher emotional intelligence to improve your relationships. When you learn how to better control your emotions, you create positive change in your life and your relationships that will not only improve them on their own but also give you other relationship benefits, such as improved empathy and trust from your partner.

Completing this chapter on self-regulation completes our discussion of personal competency, which is how aware you are of your emotions, and based on that awareness, how well you're able to predict and manage your behavior. The next chapters will deal with social competence, which is your ability to understand other peoples' emotions, behaviors, and motivations and use that information to improve your relationship.

Sharing is caring.
Let other people know that
you like this book and they will too
by **leaving a review on Amazon!**

CHAPTER 6:

SHARPENING YOUR SOCIAL AWARENESS

Social awareness (or what you might be more familiar with, empathy) is kind of like your self-awareness—only applied to other people instead of yourself. Social awareness is defined by your ability to accurately identify and understand the emotions of others. Like self-awareness, it's a foundational skill for emotional intelligence, allowing you to advance your relationships in a productive and positive direction.

As one half of the group of emotional skills we refer to as social competencies, social awareness is the half that lets you identify and understand the emotions that might be causing problems. The other half, your relationship management skills, is what allows you to act on this information and make these changes. Like self-awareness and self-regulation, we will discuss relationship management in the next chapter, after we lay out ways you can improve and utilize your social awareness.

What Role Does Social Awareness Play In Relationships?

So far, we've spent a lot of time talking about you in this book. How you feel, why you feel that way, and what you can do to control those feelings and act on them in a way that's beneficial to you and your relationship. However, relationships aren't all about you, how you feel, and what you do. There's a whole other person to think about when we're talking about improving relationships—your partner!

Like how self-awareness works for understanding yourself, social awareness is how you understand your partner. It's how you identify their emotions, see the thoughts behind them, and understand their reasons for feeling that way (even if you don't agree). Also like self-awareness, social awareness is all about listening and observing, only instead of paying attention to yourself, you're paying attention to your partner.

What A Person With High Social Awareness Looks Like:

Let's take a look at a hypothetical person with high social awareness, "Empathetic Elaine," and see what that would mean for her relationships:

- **Elaine can get along with almost anyone.** No matter where Elaine is, or who she's with, she seems to get along well with all people. She fits in at parties, is well-liked in the office, and gets along with her partner's in-laws with relative ease. This is not because she is an amazing or profoundly interesting person, it's because Elaine has a good feel for other people's personalities, and is able to act—and react—in ways these people find pleasant, appropriate and expected.

- **Elaine is good at communicating other people's feelings to a third party.** Elaine is a talented storyteller. One of her best skills is accurately communicating the feelings other people had at the time. Why So-and-So's feelings were hurt, why Steve fell in love with Sally, how Peter felt when he got that big promotion.

- **Elaine is an active listener.** When she is listening to someone talk, Elaine is very engaged. She naturally keeps welcoming body language, follows the course of the conversation well, and asks appropriate and worthwhile questions based on the context and details of the story she's being told.

Now let's look at Elaine's hypothetical counterpoint: Self-absorbed Sandra. Let's see what someone with low social awareness looks like in a relationship.

- **Sandra struggles in new social situations.** When meeting new people or going to a new place, Sandra has trouble fitting in. She struggles to read the tone of a room or setting, and will often act in ways that aren't quite appropriate, creating stress and embarrassment for herself and others.

- **Sandra is a bad listener.** For Sandra, conversations only have two parts: When she gets to talk, and when she doesn't. She always seems to be waiting to express her opinion on a given subject, and what she has to say rarely has much to do with what's being said by the other party.

- **Sandra has a hard time understanding where others are coming from.** Sandra has a rigid understanding of what's fair and unfair and has a very hard time understanding someone who doesn't agree with her. This causes a lot of problems in her current relationship, where she just can't understand why her partner has to talk to their mom so much. (Sandra only talks to her mom once a month. Why would anyone need to talk to a parent more than that?)

Strategies For Improving Your Social Awareness

Here are some strategies and tips for improving your social awareness. When you set out to use these strategies, don't forget about the self-awareness skills you picked up in Chapter Four, because being able to understand yourself is incredibly helpful when trying to understand others. Almost all of the strategies laid out below—from working on your listening skills to learning about your partner's culture and background—can be made much more effective if you're able to use your self-awareness skills to complement them.

For example, take the first strategy described below: Work on your listening skills. To complement that strategy, you can use your self-awareness skills to determine if you're in a good emotional state to be listening right now. Are you attentive and alert, or are you distracted by anger or tiredness or worrying about work? And, if you determine you're not in a good emotional state to listen, then you should use your self-regulation skills and strategies from Chapter Five to see if you can make yourself more ready to listen.

One last tip before proceeding with this chapter: Be aware that some people are just harder to understand than others. While these social-awareness skills are powerful and broadly applicable, they are by no means a perfect and complete solution for understanding other people.

This doesn't mean that if you're not connecting with someone that it's automatically their fault—no one's social awareness is perfect, and it's often reasonable to assume that there's something you can do on your side of the relationship to improve your ability to understand your partner. By saying some people are more difficult to understand than others, it means that: **Your experience and success using these tips can vary from person to person.**
It's somewhat of an obvious point to say, but people are different, and their differences play a role in how you're able

to connect with them. Part of social awareness is being able to assess those differences, but it's also important to know that your ability to assess them is not just affected by your own emotional intelligence, but by how transparent or guarded the particular person is.

Some people are very guarded and skilled at hiding their emotions, while others may be generally poor communicators, making it harder for you to listen and connect as well as you'd like. So don't worry if you feel like you've made amazing progress with your social awareness skills, but still find some people difficult to connect with—it could very well be them, and not you.

That doesn't mean that you should give up or write the person off, it just means that you'll have to work that much harder on your own social-awareness skills to connect with them.

As with the other sections, the five strategies listed below are not the only avenues for improving your social-awareness. These were selected because of their effectiveness, depth, and range for improving your social awareness.

1. Work On Your Listening Skills

One of the most important components of social awareness is your ability to listen, not just to the words your partner is saying, but how they're saying them. What are they doing with their body? Are their arms folded? Are they gesturing wildly? Did they reach out to hold your hand before talking? What about the tone of their voice? Or the speed they're talking? Are they nervously stuttering? Yelling in anger?

Improving how you pick up on these emotional cues will go a long way toward improving your social awareness. Here are some other things you can do to improve your listening skills:

- **Focus on the conversation:** This is easier said than done for some people, but do your best to listen to the conversation. Try and keep your mind from wandering, and don't worry about what you want to say next. Just keep yourself in the moment and listen to what your partner is saying to you.

- **Ask questions:** During a conversation, don't hesitate to ask questions, no matter how serious the conversation seems. Questions are a great way to increase your understanding of a given situation. Open-ended questions like, *"How did that make you feel?"* can help you gather valuable corroborating information on the situation, which will help you build more empathy and understanding with your partner. Closed-ended questions, like, *"When did this happen?"* can help you slow a conversation down and give you more time to process what's being said and give you valuable details essential to fully understanding the story.

- **Be agreeable and encouraging:** By offering small encouragements throughout the course of a conversation like, "I see your point" or "I see why you'd feel that way," you'll make your partner more comfortable and relaxed in the conversation. Once they're more comfortable and relaxed, they'll communicate more effectively, making your job of listening a whole lot easier.

2. Put Yourself In Your Partner's Shoes

"Put yourself in their shoes" is a common expression with a widely understood meaning: Step into their place and imagine things from their perspective. Next to listening, putting yourself in their shoes is one of the most important ways to increase your social awareness and is the core principal of empathy. It gives you a whole new perspective on the emotions and motivations of your partner, which in turn is invaluable for improving many elements of your relationship.

Sometimes, it can be hard, daunting, or even impossible to put yourself in your partner's shoes—especially if one or both of you are gripped deep in a serious emotional hijacking. "How could they say that?!" "I can't believe she feels that way!" "Why would he do what he did?! It's just insane!"

Take a step back, and take the emotion out of it. Think of putting yourself in their shoes as a game, like solving a puzzle, or like an acting role. Use your imagination, step out of yourself, and try and solve the mystery of your partner's behaviors.

Remember, when you're out of your shoes, and in someone else's, the goal is to think as if you were *them*—not *yourself* in their position. The only way you're going to be able to understand their perspective is if you commit to thinking about things the way they do. Use what you know about their personality, their background, and what you believe them to be feeling to give yourself the best understanding possible of why your partner is acting or feeling the way that they do.

3. Choose The "Right" Moments To Make Your Point

Just like your mood and emotions play a role in how you react to things, so to do your partner's. When you need to bring up something that may cause conflict, it's important that you're able to choose the right moments to do so.

For example, your partner just got in a knock-down, 10-alarm screaming match with her sister. Right after that fight would not be a good time bring up the controversial camping trip you want to take with your drinking buddies and your ex-girlfriend, Sensual Suzanne.

Nor would it be a good time to bring up how your mother is going to be living with you both for the next couple months. And it would be an especially bad time to point out that your partner needs to calm down, because you're really tired of listening to the complaining, and besides, you think her sister was in the right in the argument anyway.

However, that doesn't mean the above points shouldn't be discussed. They're important issues that should be addressed, they just need to be brought up at the right time, i.e. when your partner is in a reasonable emotional state to participate in a more difficult conversation.

Here are some things you can do to help identify the right moments to discuss difficult moments with your partner:

Use your listening skills. Listen to what your partner is saying, and how they're saying it. Pay attention to other cues like their body language and tone of voice. If it seems like they're not in the mood to have a serious conversation, don't try and force one.

Make small talk. Having a light conversation with your partner can be a practical way to identify their mood. Ask them about their day, about dinner, about your favorite TV show, or the latest gossip in your shared social circle and see how they react. Do they seem engaged? Or are they disinterested in topics that normally excite them? By feeling out their mood through various conversation subjects, you can get a sense of how ready they could be for a larger conversation.

Put yourself in their shoes. If you know on the surface level why your partner is upset (say for example that you were present for the blow-up fight they had with their sister), then put yourself in their shoes and think about how they're feeling right now.

If you had just a huge fight with your sister, would you be in the right mindset to have a serious conversation? Or would you be so overcome with emotion from the argument, that what you'd need most from your partner is some emotional support and understanding?

4. Learn The Rules Of Your Partner's Cultural And Socioeconomic Background

How and where people are raised affects how they express and interpret emotions. A person born to a rich Catholic family who was raised as an only child is going to have different emotional behaviors compared to someone who grew up in a poor family of seven that never really went to church.

Being able to identify and understand the emotional differences that stem from different upbringing is a core component of social awareness. Why?

Because different upbringing trains people on different emotional and social rules. Even if your partner grew up with a background largely similar to yours, there could still be socioeconomic or cultural factors creating tension in your relationship. A few examples:

- **Your partner is reluctant to move in to your apartment before marriage.** Even though you've been dating for years, they're reluctant to take the next step and move in with you, and they're not really explaining why. At first, you think it's because they're having doubts about your relationship, but then you think about their background a little.

  They grew up in a large, religious family, where every one of their older brothers and sisters got married before moving in with their partners. If they moved in with you before getting married, they'd be the first to go against this tradition, putting them in a potentially awkward situation with their family.

- **Your partner gets upset when they see you throwing away some old food that's gone bad.** You let three-quarters of a bag of vegetables go bad in your fridge. It was an honest mistake, they were just hidden behind some other items, and you didn't see them for a couple weeks. Shrugging it off, you simply threw the vegetables away.

Your partner sees this and lets out a big, disappointed sigh, and maybe even has a few words for you in a not-so-nice tone of voice. You notice this is an unusually intense reaction for a $3.00 bag of vegetables. You think it's because they're the one who paid for the vegetables but thinking about it more, you realize it's because they grew up in a poor family, where food was especially previous, so spoiled food was both rare, and a big deal if it happened.

- **Your partner takes great offense when one of your friends makes an off-hand joke about single moms.** While hanging out at a party, one of your friends makes a passing joke about single moms always being in their kids' business. Your partner jumps down your friend's throat, browbeating him over how hard single moms have it, and how he shouldn't make jokes about things he doesn't understand. While you agree that the joke was dumb, you also don't think it warranted such an intense reaction.

You first think your partner reacted that way because they're in a bad mood, and maybe even because you think they don't like your friend (he can be a bit hard to digest sometimes), but then you're able to connect her reaction to her background. Because she grew up with an overbearing single mother, you realize she's probably very sensitive about single mothers, both because she loves her mother and appreciates the things she did for her, but also because she feels some embarrassment, shame, and bitterness over some ways her overbearing mother treated her and doesn't enjoy having people remind her of it, even if it's in a simple passing joke.

The above examples are based on you knowing your partner fairly well, but what if you don't? What if you've only just met, and don't have a firm understanding of their background?

Just ask questions.

It's that simple. Take the time to ask about your partner's background and upbringing. How they grew up, where, what their siblings were like, if their parents got along, all the things you'd want to know to help you understand where they're coming from.

5. Get Opinions On Yourself From Others.

Social awareness isn't just about how you see other people—it's also about how other people see you. Understanding how people see you can not only give you important information on your behavior, it can also give you valuable information on how other people are personally interpreting your behavior.

For improving social awareness, it's the latter point of how others are interpreting your emotions and behaviors that we're talking about. For example, if you feel you come off as calm and fair in arguments, but your partner insists that you come off as condescending and snippy, who's really right?

The likely answer is that both of you are some parts correct, but that's not really a useful answer. To get closer to the truth, you may want to ask close friends how they think you come off in arguments. Do they think you're calm? Or do they think your calmness masks a quiet, sarcastic temperament?

The answer they give will help you determine your next action: If they also think you're a little mean in arguments, then your partner is right, and you need to be nicer in arguments. If the opposite is true, however, then you know that your partner is perhaps more sensitive than your friends, and you can use that information to guide future behavior with them.

> ## Practical Tip: Take An Emotional Intelligence Survey, And Ask Your Friends To Evaluate You As Well.
>
> You can actually send your close friends a survey about yourself that asks them to answer specific emotional intelligence information about yourself. Called 360-degree surveys, they're easy enough to find online. You can even take the quiz yourself, and compare your answers about yourself to what your friends say. (Often, your friends' answers turn out to be much more accurate than your own!)

Improving your social awareness is a critical part of increasing your emotional intelligence and understanding your relationships in a whole new way. By learning how to better identify the emotions and moods of others, you give yourself more opportunity to adapt to their behaviors and needs, through the final component of emotional intelligence broadly referred to as social regulation or relationship skills, which will be discussed in the following chapter.

CHAPTER 7:

STEPPING UP YOUR SOCIAL REGULATION

The fourth and final component to improving your emotional intelligence is social regulation—your ability to use the information you're getting from both your self-awareness and your social awareness to successfully manage your relationships. This component of emotional intelligence is also sometimes referred to as social skills or relationship management. For the purposes of this book, however, we'll be using the term "social regulation" to match with its sister term from Chapter Five, self-regulation.

Social regulation is the second half of your social competencies, the first being social awareness. Social regulation allows you to act on the information you've gained from social awareness, in order to improve your relationships. It can also help you free someone from emotional hijacking—only this time the person you're removing is your partner, and not yourself.

Unlike the other three components of emotional intelligence, social regulation fully depends on your abilities in the other three areas—self-awareness, self-regulation, and social awareness. This is because, as you probably now know, to affect change in a relationship, you not only have to understand your partner but also yourself.

Why Social Regulation Is Important To Emotional Intelligence And Improving Your Relationships

Social Regulation is important to your relationships because, in many ways, it *is* your relationship. How you interact, understand, and communicate with your partner is more or less how a relationship is defined. So, while self-regulation, and self- and social-awareness are extremely important to your emotional intelligence and your relationship, social regulation is all about the relationship itself, i.e., how you and your partner are working together to enjoy your time together.

What A Person With High Social Regulation Looks Like:

Let's look at another hypothetical person, and see what high social regulation skills look like in a relation, with "Successful Stan":

- **Successful Stan is understanding.** Everyone who spends time with Stan comes away with the feeling that he understands them. People feel listened to, and also that Stan is legitimately interested in what's going on in their life. He's someone people can talk to about their problems and receive fair advice when they want it, and consolation and support when they don't.

- **Successful Stan is level-headed.** Even in times of stress, Stan seems to keep his cool. His level-head has been very valuable in his relationships, allowing him to have hard conversations and handle bad news with little difficulty or emotional hijacking.

- **Successful Stan has a great marriage.** Stan has been married for over 25 years. While his marriage has had its ups and downs, overall, people describe his relationship with his partner as idyllic. And while Stan's partner would never describe him has perfect, they do feel a very strong sense of connection and trust with him. They may fight now and again, but there are few persistent arguments or long-term problems that cannot be solved.

Now let's look at our last hypothetical person, "Frustrating Frank," and see what low social regulation looks like in a relationship:

- **Frustrating Frank is tough to be around.** Frank has a terrible habit of making every conversation about him. He's a poor listener and struggles to read the mood of the room. He tells jokes at the wrong time, and is constantly talking over, or even yelling at, people to get his opinions heard.

- **Frustrating Frank is moody beyond belief.** Frank seems to have no control of his emotions, and has a habit of letting his feelings steer him down whatever path they happen to lead him down. Even worse, Frank takes his negative emotions out on others, often blaming them for his feelings, even when they're not at fault.

- **Frustrating Frank has a hard time with long-term relationships.** Frank is able to date and meet new people with some success. However, as soon as a relationship hits its first rough patch, Frank is out the door. He seems unwilling, or even unable, to resolve conflict in a way that would preserve his relationships.

Strategies For Improving Your Social Regulation

Let's look at some strategies for improving your social regulation abilities. To do these well, you're going to need your other three emotional intelligence skills, so come prepared!

Some of the strategies in this section are a little longer and more in depth than in the other sections. We're tackling some more complicated strategies in this section, such as having a difficult conversation with your partner. That's because social regulation is where the more complex work gets done in improving relationships.

Think of it this way: Understanding and managing the emotions of one person is difficult on its own (we spent two chapters on it), but adding another person to the situation makes it much more complicated. That's not to say that it's more difficult—or that you should be worried in any way— just that some of these strategies are inherently more complex than those that appear in the other chapters.

Like with the other three EI skills, don't be put off if you don't immediately adjust to social-regulation. This is undoubtedly the most difficult one of the four components of emotional intelligence to master. Not only does succeeding in it require you to have excellent social awareness, self-regulation, and self-awareness, but it also demands the same from the other person in the relationship! So, it's important to remember that not everyone's emotional intelligence is the same (nor a good match for yours). As a result, some interactions and relationships can be more difficult than others.

But, always remember, difficulty doesn't necessarily mean it's time to give up. Sometimes, you just need to intensify your efforts or try a new approach to make progress with someone you're having a little more trouble connecting with than normal.

Social regulation is an absolutely massive topic, and because of its importance in relationships, has been explored and researched in great depth. The five strategies below are far from the only ways you can approach improving your self-regulation skills.

There is a wealth of information out there on the subject. We selected these five topics for similar reasons as we did for the other three chapters: These strategies are high-impact, foundational skills that will give you a diverse and sturdy foundation for improving your social regulation.

1. In Arguments, Offer Solutions

When you're in the throes of an argument with your partner, sometimes the last thing you want to do is give up on trying to prove you're right and instead offer a solution to the problem your partner is facing. But to improve your emotional intelligence in your relationship, you must be prepared to do exactly this.

Take a step back and think about it this way. Say you're at a fast-food restaurant, and the clerk at the counter has gotten your order wrong and given you the wrong food. You approach the clerk with the wrong order and point out his mistake.

Now, the clerk is pretty positive that your order is correct, and that you just accidentally ordered something you didn't want. However, even if the clerk is positive that is the case—that you really did order wrong—he'll never point that out to you, the customer. Instead, he'll offer a solution—after a quick apology, he'll fix your order and ask the kitchen to make you what you really wanted, free of charge.

Why does the fast food clerk do this? Because who cares who's right or wrong in this situation? The clerk wants to keep you as a customer, and it takes almost no effort or expense to correct the order. Even though the clerk is almost positive that you ordered incorrectly, and he could argue that point if he wanted to, doing so would be counterproductive to his goals of keeping you as a customer and maintaining that relationship.

Now, that is a bit of a simplistic example. Certainly, most relationship arguments are not as simple or low stakes as an argument in a fast-food restaurant. However, two core points from the above example carry over perfectly for relationships:

- **You gain nothing by fighting over who's correct and who's incorrect this very second.** There are exceptions to this rule, but for the most part, "who's right and who's wrong" conversations rarely succeed when they've escalated into full-blown arguments. Instead, all each side really achieves is adding more stress and baggage into a relationship. So if there's nothing to gain besides a small victory for your pride, and there's plenty to lose, why even bother fighting about it?

- **Offering solutions reduces tensions, builds trust, and sometimes ends the argument outright.** After the fast food clerk corrected your order, would you continue to complain to him about the initial order being wrong? Probably not, because what would be the point?

Now, the solution you offer may not be as complete and cut-and-dry as a fixed food order, but applying the same principle can lead to similar results. For example, if you're fighting about your weekend plans, you could offer to spend time with your partner's family this weekend, and let them know that next weekend, you'd like to go out with your friends. After all, does it really matter who's right about where your social time should be spent, if you're both getting something you want out of the solution?

2. Have The Tough Conversations

We've alluded to tough conversations throughout this book. Now that we've built up some emotional intelligence tools, it's time to talk about how to actually have them. Here are some strategies you can use to make your touchy conversations easier to have, smoother to experience, and ending with better emotional results for both you and your partner.

Start On Common Ground.

Tough conversations tend to go better if you and partner begin from a point of agreement. It builds a sense of trust and involvement, helping your partner feel like you're both on the same team, and also that you have shared stakes in the conversation.

Sometimes a common ground is easy to find (*"We both know our relationship has been struggling for a little while*" or "*You know that I love you*"). But that's not always the case. If you're struggling to find common ground, consider making the conversation itself the point of common ground. "*Thanks for talking with me about this. I know it's going to be hard for you too.*" Saying that or something similar can be an effective way to create a sense of common ground.

Ask To Hear Their Side Of The Issue First.

It may seem counterintuitive for you to start a tough conversation by asking your partner to tell you how they feel about it first, but there are a couple reasons to handle the conversation this way.

First, it lets you avoid any frustration they might have about not having a chance to put their side of the story out there. If you allow them to begin the conversation with their chance to be heard, they'll not only feel better, but be more likely to let you speak your piece uninterrupted in return.

Second, hearing their side of the story before you go into your explanation of the issue will allow you to adjust what you were going to say to include points from their story. ("*You mentioned that you were especially hurt when you found out I went through your text history. I can see why you feel that way, and I think that's fair. I went through it because…*")

Adjusting your conversation this way will make your partner feel more included and heard. In turn, it will help you take the conversation in the direction you want it to go.

Resist The Urge To Argue Against Their Points.

When your partner is explaining their side of the issue, use your self-management skills to avoid correcting or arguing with them. You're going to get your chance to speak, and you letting your partner speak first was not to see if they agree to your version of the truth.

You're trying to understand where they're coming from, and why they feel the way they do. You also want them to feel heard, and you want to improve your own understanding of the issue. This not the time to prove the details of your story right, and theirs wrong.

Explain Your Side Of The Issue, So They're Able To Understand It.

When describing your side of the issue, make sure that you're doing it in a way that makes the what's, why's, and how's clear and understandable to your partner. Don't just give all the details and pain points of what you're feeling.

Do so in a way that they'll understand. Be clear, be direct, but most importantly, use your social awareness to take what you know about your partner and present details to them in a way they'll best understand. Sometimes, not much communication work is necessary, because it's easy to make your point. (*"You really hurt my feelings when I caught you texting your ex."*) Other times, you may have to more carefully and thoroughly frame your point to make it clear. (*"I know you love your mom, and I do too, but sometimes I struggle to spend long periods of time with her. I didn't grow up with a talkative mom like you did, so it's a little more difficult for me to spend time with someone who talks so much. It's nothing against her, it's just ... different for me. I'm not used to answering so many questions from a parental figure, and it makes me nervous. Not because I think your mom is going to pass judgment on me for anything, although that is a small concern, but because my parents were very judgmental, so I feel this innate fearful twisting in my gut whenever a parental figure asks me questions. Does this make sense?*)

Do What You Can To Resolve The Issue, Or At Least Move It Forward.

Once you both understand each other's side of the issue, it's time to actually resolve it. If you can't resolve it now, at least move it forward. That depends on the actual issue at hand.

However, when moving toward a resolution, try to use inclusive language that continues to create common ground ("We probably shouldn't date anymore" vs. "I'm leaving you") and be sure to ask for your partner's feelings after you announce the decision you'd like to make ("We probably shouldn't date anymore. Do you feel the same way?")

Check In Afterward.

Depending on the issue you were working on, you may want to check in with your partner to see how they're feeling about the decision. If, for example, you decided to quit your full-time job to pursue freelance photography, even if your partner was okay with the decision at the time, you might want to check in again after the first cycle of bills hits, to see if they're still feeling as good when less money is coming in.

Checking in will not only show that you care, but also allow you to check if your partner has any changes in emotion since you last made the decision together. That can help alleviate any potential pent up negative emotions that could result in future emotional blowups.

3. Use Complementary Behavior To Help Ease Tense Situations With Your Partner.

By complementary behavior, we don't mean complimenting your partner with kindnesses, like telling them how attractive they are. Though they sound similar, it's actually a different word we're using: complement, meaning "to complete or fill out."

The strategy we're discussing here is how picking behavior that complements your partner's current mood can be an effective way to diffuse tense or difficult situations.

For example, your partner is in a rush to get out the door to work on time. They're panicked, and upset about being late and possibly getting in real trouble with their boss. In their hurry, they ask you for help packing up their lunch. Knowing that your partner is upset and in a rush, you choose to behave in a way that complements their mood. You spring up, quickly but calmly, and sling together a lunch for them as fast as you can. Your partner appreciates the speed and seriousness and gives you a quick kiss on the check as they hurry out the door.

What makes this behavior "complementary" and not "mirroring" is that it's not an exact match to their behavior. You have hurried to put the lunch together, but you were not in a panicked rush like your partner was at that time. Had you chosen to mirror their behavior in that way, you would have made the situation worse by adding more anxiety and chaos to an already tense situation.

Similarly, had you chosen the uncomplimentary behavior, say by telling them to relax and that it was no big deal if they had to buy lunch today, you also would have made the situation worse by invalidating their feelings and presenting yourself as an obstacle to them achieving their goals, instead of being an asset.

This is why the complementary behavior is so helpful in diffusing situations like these—it shows your partner that you understand the immediate need and vibe of the current situation, and also that you're part of their emotional support system, someone they can count on to back them up when things get tough.

4. Be Accessible (But Don't Be Afraid To Set Boundaries Too.)

It's important that your partner feel comfortable talking about their feelings with you, both in general and specifically about your relationship. To accommodate that need, you want to make yourself accessible and open to conversation. This means responding to your partner's requests to talk with calmness, friendliness, and patience. Hear them out, even if it's not exactly what you want to be doing at the moment.

Put yourself in their shoes. They may see you there, watching TV or trying to get some extra work done on your laptop, but what they want to talk to you about is really important, and they'd really feel much better if they got it off their chest now. From that perspective, you can see how important it is that you meet their requests to talk with openness and accessibility.

That's not to say that you can't have boundaries. You're entitled to have places and/or times where you don't want to have a serious talk. Just be sure that you're consistent with those boundaries, and that those boundaries are fair to you and your partner. For example, you may have a boundary that you can't really talk on the phone at work unless it's an emergency, but you can message each other throughout the day.

5. Express Even Small Displays Of Gratitude To Make A Big Difference.

We'll end our emotional intelligence strategies with something simple, yet important—expressing even small displays of gratitude can make a big difference in your relationship. Whether it's showing that you care with small, thoughtful gifts and gestures, or it's staying on top of basic relationship courtesies like remembering to say *please* and *thank you*, these little gestures can go a long way toward building trust, affection, and goodwill with your partner.

When you're in a relationship with someone for a long time, especially when you're living with them, it can be easy to forget common formal politeness, because your relationship isn't formal and proper—it's fun and warm and comfortable and full of love. However, just because you can relax around your partner, doesn't mean that they don't enjoy hearing the word *thank you* for a favor or nice gesture. In fact, when a thank you comes from someone they love, they might even enjoy hearing it more!

This strategy might seem small, but it's very effective in building mutual respect between partners. While large, sweeping emotional gestures can have a very big positive impact on a relationship (helping a partner move, going all out for Valentine's Day, showing up when they called in sick from work and nursing them back to health), these things don't happen very often.

So, relationships depend on these small gestures of affection, respect, and kindness to set the tone and let each person know how the other feels about them. In many ways, they're an essential form of communication in relationships. So be sure to put these kinds of affectionate and polite communications out there to show your partner how you feel about them.

CHAPTER 8:

PUTTING IT ALL TOGETHER

Now that we've gone over the four parts of emotional intelligence—social regulation, social awareness, self-regulation, and self-awareness—and presented strategies for improving each, let's put what you've learned together and practice solving some hypothetical relationship problems. It'll be a great way to reinforce what you've learned, as well as improve your emotional intelligence that much further.

Each of these exercises can have multiple solutions. There's no one right answer because that's not the idea here. The idea is for you to use what you've learned and see if you can use it to create a solution that you think would work best.

One last bit of advice before you jump into the exercises: Remember—the four core emotional intelligence skills are intertwined with one another. You must use all four components to come to the solutions you think will work best. So don't hesitate to go back and review the chapters if you need a refresher on any of the four key component skills.

What You'll Need For These Exercises:

Paper and a writing tool

Or

If you're reading this book on your phone, open a notetaking app, and mark your answers there. You could also use a Word document if you're reading on your laptop or desktop.

The Four Emotional Intelligence Categories And Accompanying Strategies At A Glance

Self-Awareness

- Stop judging your feelings
- Pay attention to your negative emotions
- Don't let your current mood control you
- Learn your triggers
- Connect with your physical side

Self-Regulation

- Diffuse negative emotions by adding time
- Control how you talk to yourself
- Create more emotional control by harnessing the power of positivity
- Get an outside perspective from someone else
- Learn to accept—and expect—change

Social Awareness

- Work on your listening skills
- Put yourself in your partner's shoes
- Choose the right moments to make your point
- Learn the rules of your partner's cultural and socioeconomic background
- Get opinions on yourself from others

Social Regulation

- In arguments, offer solutions
- Have tough conversations
- Use complementary behavior to help ease tense situations
- Be accessible
- Express even small displays of gratitude to make a big difference

Exercise 1: A Partner Suddenly Has To Work Late

Workaholic Wendy texts her husband, Put-Upon Preston, late on a Friday afternoon. It turns out she's got to work late, and won't be home until much later that night—maybe not until ten o'clock.

Preston is furious. Not only did Wendy promise to bring home dinner for him and their kids, but she was also supposed to watch the kids for a bit while Preston ran out to the store and picked up some groceries for the weekend. Now, Preston is left scrambling to come up with a replacement dinner for himself and the kids and is also going to have to wake up early and run out to the grocery store on a Saturday morning—one of the busiest and most annoying times to go.

And on top of that, he was also looking forward to spending some time with his wife tonight. Now, he's not even going to see her until late, and who knows if she's going to even want to talk when she gets home. Often when Wendy works late, she comes home burnt-out, tired, and grumpy. She usually just sits on her phone for an hour, maybe watches a little TV, then goes to bed spaced out, still in a daze from working so many hours.

The worst part of all of this for Preston is that this has been happening several times a week, for months—always with short notice, and rarely with more than a quick "Sorry!" through a text. Wendy makes a lot of money at her job and is a very career-driven person.

Preston has to admit that her career success has done their marriage and family a lot of good—they've never wanted for anything and are comfortably saving money—but Preston is starting to wonder if the money is really worth it. He's really struggling to keep up with plans always changing at the last minute and with a lot of the child and home care work being dumped on his lap.

He misses his wife and how they used to be able to spend time together. They've been married for years, and Preston truly loves Wendy, but he's at a total loss for how to solve this situation, let alone tell her how he feels about her workaholism.

If you were Preston, how would you go about resolving this situation with Wendy? Take some time to write out what you'd do, starting with self-awareness action items, then progressing through the other three key emotional intelligence components.

IDEAS TO EXPLORE & INFORM YOUR ANSWERS

What self-awareness skills could Preston use to help himself understand his feelings about this situation?

- Could Preston's angry mood be getting the best of him? Is he more angry at the principle of the situation (being ignored and cast aside again) than the practical reality of the issue (ordering pizza is a completely easy and reasonable solution for a quick dinner, and it's far from the end of the world to have to go grocery shopping on a Saturday morning).

- Is the habitual cancellation of plans making this more angering than normal? Is it something that's becoming "triggering" for him? If it is becoming triggering, what are some things Preston can do to control these feelings?

- What can Preston's anger and hurt over these continuously canceled plans tell him about how feels about their relationship? And how closely aligned with reality are these feelings? Is he really doing the majority of the child and home care, or does it just feel that way sometimes, especially when plans are canceled?

How can Preston use social awareness to understand Wendy's perspective in this situation?

- How has work been going for Wendy overall? Preston knows she's been busy, but he admits he doesn't know many details past that. Would he feel better if he knew more about why she was staying so late all the time? Should he take some time to talk to her about work?

- Related to the above, how is Wendy feeling overall? She's been missing a lot of family time with working late so much. Preston knows she loves him and the kids, but Wendy tends to keep her emotions close, and doesn't really share her feelings unless Preston really digs. Could Wendy be really bothered by working late so often, or does it not bother her?

- When should Preston choose to have a hard conversation with Wendy about her constant, last-minute lateness? Right when she gets back home from working a 13-hour day in the office, or some time tomorrow when they've both had a little rest and time away from the situation?

What self-regulation skills could Preston use to help manage his feelings and behavior?

- What role is Preston's self-talk playing in making the situation worse? Currently, he's very upset, berating himself up over and over for being such a pushover, and for not having a better job himself (maybe then Wendy wouldn't have to work so hard).

- Are there any positive results here that Preston could be focusing on? He gets to spend some one-on-one bonding time with his kids, which is something he always enjoys. He's also reasonably justified to splurge on dinner—maybe he could get fancy pizza from the gourmet brick-oven place down the street. He could even order something for Wendy when she gets home.

- Should Preston accept Wendy's need to work late as a temporary truth of their marriage? While it's true that Wendy could maybe give him more notice, or at least not make definite plans if there's a chance she's going to cancel them, would Wendy really work late so much for no reason? Her career has been going great, could her schedule be a temporary birthing pain of her advancing career?

How can Preston use social regulation to try and resolve the issues here?

- Are there any solutions or compromises Preston could offer to help ease the situation? Is there anything he could do to help Wendy spend less time in the office? Maybe he could make her lunches, so she doesn't have to spend precious time in the office looking for food? Or could he do something that would help her leave earlier in the morning so she can make it home earlier?

  And what about solutions from Wendy? Would Preston feel better about Wendy canceling if she also offered a solution, such as, "I'm going to be home late again, but I called my mother, and she's going to come over and help with the kids so you can still make it to the store"?

- Even though he doesn't really feel like it, would it be helpful in resolving the issue by thanking Wendy for working so hard for their family? After all, a 13-hour day is nothing to sneeze at.

- When it comes time to have a conversation about Wendy's habitual lateness, does Preston have a plan? Does he know what he wants to say? What common ground could he build between them both on this specific issue?

Exercise 2: Fighting Over Cleaning The Apartment

Messy Mike and Clean Calvin have been living together for a couple years. Their relationship was great when they had separate apartments, but now that they live together, Calvin is having a lot of trouble with Mike's messiness. He loves Mike, but he's not sure how much longer he can take it.

It's not just that Mike is super-messy—though he is—it's that his messiness all seems so needless and, well, lazy, to Calvin. Mike's dishes never seem to make it to the sink, let alone get rinsed off. They just pile up wherever Mike finished eating, scraps of food still on them and all. Mike always seems to be starting laundry, but never finishes it. There is always wet clothing in the washer, dry clothes in the dryer, and piles of unorganized clothes everywhere. Calvin isn't even sure which piles are clean and which piles are dirty.

The worst part for Calvin though is that Mike never wants to help clean the apartment when they have guests coming over. It always falls on Calvin to not only pick up after Mike—all his dishes and his clothes—but also to do all the rest of the cleaning in the apartment: mopping the floors, vacuuming, wiping down the kitchen, and straightening up. It's not a big apartment, but it's still a lot of work, taking Calvin several hours every week.

Calvin has tried to bring it up to Mike a couple times, but every time Mike has been very hostile, telling him to get off his back and to stop trying to control him. Their last argument about cleaning got pretty heated, and Calvin is a little nervous about bringing it up again. He knows he has to though, he just has no idea how to go about it.

If you were Calvin, how would you go about resolving this situation with Mike? Take some time to write out what you'd do, starting with self-awareness action items, then progressing through the other three key emotional intelligence components.

IDEAS TO EXPLORE & INFORM YOUR ANSWERS

What self-awareness skills could Calvin use to help himself understand his feelings about this situation?

- Whenever Calvin has to clean up after Mike, he gets so swept up in the moment (no pun intended) that he's doesn't focus much on how he's feeling. He's always in a rush to clean and prefers to focus on getting the cleaning done as fast as possible, rather than thinking about how he feels. What could Calvin do to pay better attention to his feelings?

- Calvin always feels very guilty about getting upset about having a messy house. He knows it bothers Mike when he complains about it, and he also feels it's uncool and lame to be such a neat freak. What can Calvin do to be less judgmental about his feelings?

- What can Calvin's feelings about the situation tell him about himself and his relationship with Mike? Why is he dreading having a simple conversation about cleaning? What does that say about him, and what could he do to change for the better?

How can Calvin use social awareness to understand Mike's perspective in this situation?

- Why is Mike so messy? Has he been like this his whole life? Calvin thinks about what he knows about Mike's childhood and doesn't think he could have been as messy then. Mike's mother has a very strong personality, and based on what Calvin has seen of her and Mike's relationship, they would have fought constantly and aggressively about every little piece of trash.

- When they've fought previously about cleaning, Mike has said "get off my back" and "stop trying to control me." Those are pretty self-explanatory statements, but they're also pretty aggressive and dramatic considering it's just a conversation about cleaning up dishes and laundry. What could be making Mike react that way?

Is he an inherently dramatic person, or could Calvin be pushing Mike's buttons in other ways that are making him react that way?

- Sometimes Calvin wonders if Mike really is that messy, or if it's him that is a clean freak. They are in their early 20s after all—most men their age aren't known for their cleanliness. Is there a way Calvin could get an answer to this question?

What self-regulation skills could Calvin use to help manage his feelings and behavior?

- What role is Calvin's passive aggressive self-talk playing in making the situation worse? Whenever he's cleaning, Calvin quite literally talks to himself, saying things out loud like, "Oh, I guess I'll just do it all! I'll clean the whole place because I'm your personal maid. That's me, Cleaning Calvin, the live-in maid." Whether Mike hears Calvin when he talks to himself like this or not, he doesn't react. He just stares at the TV, his jaw tightly set.

- Are there any positive results here that Calvin could be focusing on? Certainly having to clean up after your partner is terrible, but is Mike doing anything positive that Calvin could focus on? Is he doing the cooking? Paying more than his share of the bills? Is he wonderful to spend time with when they're not fighting about cleaning?

- Calvin knows this one-sided cleaning situation is not sustainable. Eventually, it may come down to this cleaning problem getting solved, or Calvin walking out. Calvin absolutely does not want to break up, which means the cleaning situation has to get solved. What can he do to prepare for that emotionally?

How can Calvin use social regulation to try and resolve the issues here?

- When arguing about cleaning, are there solutions Calvin could offer Mike that could help ease the tension? Is there anything Calvin could do to make cleaning easier for Mike? Are there other chores that Calvin could suggest that Mike do instead of cleaning?

- Because their last few fights on the subject have been so bad, Calvin has shut himself off from talking about it. After calming down himself, Mike has approached Calvin a few times to talk about things, but before anything happens, Calvin makes an excuse, like having to run off for a time-sensitive errand. What could Calvin do differently here?

- How can Calvin plan for this hard conversation? What can he do to create common ground between them? How can he make sure that Mike feels heard?

Exercise 3: Asking To Be Exclusive, Or "Officially" Becoming A Couple

Singular Sasha and Free-Rolling Fred have been seeing each other for a couple months, maybe going on 15 or so dates over the course of that time. Things are going great.

They're having fun, really clicking and getting along well. There's only one problem: when they started dating, neither was looking for anything serious, but now, Sasha wants to take the next step and become an official couple.

When Sasha and Fred started dating, they were both committed to being single, not interested in having a serious relationship of any kind. Both of them were seeing other people. Both knew that and were okay with that arrangement, at least at the beginning. Now though, Sasha thinks she's developing more serious feelings for Fred, and she wants more than their current casual arrangement.

She wants to spend more time with Fred. She wants him to meet her friends and family. And most of all, she doesn't want to share him with other women anymore. Her problem is, she's not sure if Fred is on the same page.

Fred and Sasha haven't had many serious conversations, but from the few serious talks they have had, Sasha feels like Fred is not interested in settling down. He's said that he recently got out of a long-term relationship about a year ago, and he'd been with that person for almost ten years. The breakup was painful and took a long time to resolve and heal. Fred has said that for now, he's really not interested in anything serious. He's just not ready.

Only Sasha thinks he seems ready. He's getting more affectionate the more they see each other and is suggesting activities that are less like "dates' and more like "couples activities" like going with him to the farmer's market on Sunday morning or meeting up at the gym to work out together a bit before going to work. He's bringing her small silly gifts, like little sentimental pieces of memorabilia from their earlier dates, and they're starting to text back and forth during the day just for fun.

Sasha is feeling very confused and has no idea what to do. On the one hand, she feels like Fred was very clear about his desire to not have a serious relationship. She doesn't want to say that's not good enough for her and risk losing what they currently have together.

But on the other hand, he said that very early on when they were dating, so maybe he doesn't mean it anymore? Also, he certainly isn't acting like he only wants something casual. Some days, Sasha feels like they're already an actual couple.

Sasha knows she has to address this with Fred soon. Her feelings for him are only getting stronger. But, she's very afraid of risking the relationship by putting herself out there and making it clear that she wants more than Fred may be willing to offer.

If you were Sasha, how would you go about resolving this situation with Fred? Take some time to write out what you'd do, starting with self-awareness action items, then progressing through the other three key emotional intelligence components.

IDEAS TO EXPLORE & INFORM YOUR ANSWERS

What self-awareness skills could Sasha use to help herself understand her feelings about this situation?

- This problem with Fred is making Sasha crazy. She's losing sleep over her fear of losing him and is starting to feel guilty every time she sees him because she feels like she's lying to him—pretending to feel one way, while actually feeling another. What could she do to help acknowledge these feelings, without torturing herself with them?

- Thinking about the mixed signals that Fred has been sending her, Sasha is wondering if *she* has been sending mixed signals to *him*. Since she's realized her feelings for Fred, how has she been acting? Has she been too standoffish for fear of losing him? Or too affectionate, which risks revealing her true feelings? What is the best way for her to act?

- What can Sasha learn about herself from her fear of losing Fred? Is this fear just about losing Fred, or does she have trouble speaking her mind in other tough situations? If it's the latter, what does that mean for Sasha? What could she do to become more comfortable with speaking her mind?

How can Sasha use social awareness to understand Fred's recent behavior and figure out if he's interested in a more serious relationship or not?

- Sasha isn't sure if she's reading too much into Fred's recent romantic gestures or not. What are some ways she could analyze Fred's behavior to really pin down and define his mood and feelings in a given moment?

For example, when they go to the Farmer's market next Sunday morning, what should Sasha look for in Fred to see if he's interested in dating her more seriously? Could she put herself in his shoes, and think about what he would do if he were trying to convince her to date him more seriously?

- What's a good time for Sasha to pick to have this conversation with Fred? Should she just blurt it out on one of their next dates, or should she try and pick an optimal time and location to have the conversation? If it's the latter, what times and places would be good, and why?

- Sasha has kept her problems with Fred to herself. She's starting to feel very alone and trapped in her own head. What could she do to alleviate these feelings? And in the future, what could she do to realize she's feeling trapped in her head in the first place? Are these feelings affecting her behavior around Fred or the way he receives her lately?

What self-regulation skills could Sasha use to help manage her feelings and behavior?

- Sasha is very tied up in thinking about the worst-case scenario of her and Fred breaking up. What are some positives that she could focus on instead? What would it mean if Fred is interested in a more serious relationship, but is also afraid to bring it up?

- Every time Sasha sees Fred, she gets swept up in her emotions and is completely hijacked by her strong affection for him. How can Sasha create some distance from her emotions and actually come to a rational decision about what she wants to say to Fred?

- Can Sasha emotionally prepare for the worst-case scenario, which is Fred and her breaking up because he doesn't want a more serious relationship? What would the breakup mean for Sasha?

How can Sasha use social regulation to try and resolve the issue with Fred?

- How can Sasha adjust the signals she's sending Fred to make sure that 1) It seems like she's open and receptive to his increased affection and 2) She seems open to serious conversation about their relationship status?

- How can Sasha plan for the conversation about their relationship status with Fred? Since they talked a little bit about their relationship goals and desires when they first started dating, could a follow up on that conversation be a good starting point? Or, would you approach the conversation differently?

- Is Sasha giving Fred the right feedback for all the small affectionate gestures he's paying her? What could she do to make sure that she's showing appropriate gratitude? What value would showing that gratitude have?

Exercise 4: What Happens When Mom-In-Law Keeps Asking For Money?

Cashed-Out Carrie and Loyal Laura have a problem: Laura's mom keeps asking the couple for money, and it's really starting to bother Carrie. The couple has been married for a few years, and they've been living together for even longer. They combined their finances years ago, which had been working out great until the problem with Laura's mom popped up.

Laura's mom always seems to need money. Sixty dollars here. Two-fifty there. Once or twice, she asked for $1,500. It has been going on for years, and it's really starting to add up and affect the couple's finances. Laura doesn't seem to mind—she's just glad she's able to help her mom, but Carrie is not sure how much longer she can take it.

Carrie knows that she should feel more sympathy for Laura's mom. She's an older woman who's been single for a long time, and through a mix of poor health and bad luck, has had trouble holding down a career. She was very good to Laura as a child, making sure she had the best childhood possible.

But now, it feels like their roles have flipped and Laura is spending all her time and resources caring for her mother. Laura's mother is only 63, which Carrie feels is young enough that she should be able to take care of herself but that's not the real issue.

What upsets Carrie the most is that Laura's mother always says she'll pay back the money, but never does. She just takes more and more money, with barely a thank you, as if she's entitled to it because she's Laura's mother.

Carrie has brought up her feelings about this situation with Laura's mom a few times, and it has not gone well. Laura is very protective and defensive about her mother and doesn't see any other option besides giving her the money she needs. While Carrie isn't suggesting that Laura cut her mother off, she also doesn't see how these constant micro-loans can possibly be necessary unless Laura's financial skills are just ridiculously stupid. She's a grown woman, there's no reason she should need to "borrow" $60 every two weeks. The argument usually escalates from there, ending in a big fight with one of them sleeping on the couch.

Carrie is at a loss for what to do. She knows she has to figure out how to fix this problem in their relationship with some kind of compromise, but she has no idea how to come up with one that will make them both happy. She doesn't even know how to start the conversation. Every time she's tried, it's ended in a big fight that just made everything worse.

If you were Carrie, how would you go about resolving this situation with Laura and her mother? Take some time to write out what you'd do, starting with self-awareness action items, then progressing through the other three key emotional intelligence components.

IDEAS TO EXPLORE & INFORM YOUR ANSWERS

What self-awareness skills could Carrie use to help herself understand her feelings about this situation?

- Every time Carrie thinks about this lending situation with Laura and her mom, she becomes completely overwhelmed with anger. She loses all ability to think about anything else, and finds herself seething for hours. What are some strategies Carrie can use to acknowledge her anger, without becoming overwhelmed by it?

- How can Carrie use this problem with Laura and her mom to learn more about herself and her own emotions? Is she just upset about the money that's being lost, or could she have other issues?

  Could part of her anger be about Laura being very tight with money when it's Carrie who wants to spend it, but then Laura doesn't have a problem lending her mother money, no questions asked. If that's the case, what should Carrie do about those feelings?

- Carrie is starting to notice other things related to Laura's mom or money that are starting to set her off. She dislikes looking at her bank account because it always reminds her of the money they're losing. She has trouble going to family events with her in-laws because it's getting very hard to be around her mother-in-law. Is there anything Carrie can do about these triggering events, or are they just a sign of how badly Carrie needs to resolve this problem?

How can Carrie use social awareness to understand Laura's perspective on the situation?

- Carrie was never as close to her mother as Laura is with hers. But, she knows it's not uncommon. She's thinking about asking her friend Ben about his relationship with his parents. She's known Ben for a long time and knows that he's very close to his mother.

  What are some questions Carrie could ask Ben about his relationship with his mother that could be helpful in understanding Laura's relationship with her mother? Could she ask for other advice too, like how she could cope with such a difficult in-law situation?

- How does this argument look from Laura's perspective? How would it make her feel that giving a little extra money to her mother every month frustrates her partner of many years? What about the point that the conversations about loaning money always turn into a yelling match, with Laura feeling like she's not being heard?

- Laura was solely raised by her mother for almost her entire life, of which Carrie is aware. They had very little money, but Laura's mom made sure that what money they did have was spent on Laura. Carrie knows these financial hardships made mother and daughter very close, and she sees that Laura's mom has made tremendous sacrifices for her daughter in the past with no hesitation. What else could this fact tell Carrie about her partner's emotions toward her mother?

What self-regulation skills could Carrie use to help manage her feelings and behavior?

- Carrie is legitimately worried that they're going to start missing bill payments because of the money they're giving Laura's mom, apart from all the sleep she's losing over it. What are some strategies Carrie can use to make herself feel better about her financial stress or to help herself sleep better?

- Instead of letting her anger bubble up, is there anything positive about this situation that Carrie could focus on? How does it make her feel that Laura is so loving and loyal to her mother?

- When Carrie is feeling hijacked by her emotions of anger, what are some strategies she can use to help break free? How can she use the time to separate herself from the overwhelming feelings of anger so she can have the opportunity to think of solutions to their argument?

How can Carrie use social regulation to try and resolve this issue with Laura?

- Are there any compromises or solutions that Carrie could propose that could help take some of the tension and anger out of the argument? Or, what are some reasonable concessions she should expect Laura to make that could ease their disagreement?

- Every time Carrie and Laura talk about the problem, it quickly leads to a fight. What can Carrie do to keep the conversation from escalating into a fight the next time? And if a fight does happen—what can Carrie do to diffuse the situation?

- When it comes time to have this conversation, how much practical information should Carrie prepare? Is it important for her to know the exact amount of money that they've lent Laura's mother, or will that information only make the conversation worse? How can she create a sense of common ground between herself and Laura?

CONCLUSION

Great job. You have now made it through to the end of *Couples Guide To Emotional Intelligence*. Let's hope it was informative and able to provide you with all of the tools you need to achieve your goals of making your relationships more enjoyable, more stable, and longer lasting.

Keep in mind all the lessons you've learned from this book. You've learned the scientific history of emotional intelligence, gaining an appreciation for its place and importance in psychological discourse and study. You learned just what emotional intelligence is, and why it's a critical skill needed for improving your relationship. Lastly, you studied the four core components of emotional intelligence and learned strategies on how to apply them in your life. Then, everything was concluded with some exercises at the end of the book, letting you put everything you learned into practice.

The next step is to put the strategies, tips, and habits you've learned in this book into practice yourself in your current relationship! So get out there and impress your partner with your new-found sense of self-awareness, wow them with your improved ability to regulate your emotions, dazzle them with your deeper empathy and understanding of their feelings, and make them fall in love with you all over again with your increased skill in cooperating, understanding, and managing your relationship!

If you found this book useful in any way, please leave a review on Amazon letting us know how much you loved it!

Be on the lookout for more books by Jamie Bryce on Amazon and Audible.

ENNEAGRAM FOR COUPLES:

The Comprehensive Guide To Understanding Yourself And Your Partner, And Improving Your Relationship

STEVEN MILES

CONTENTS

Introduction

Congratulations! Thank you for purchasing this book. You have just purchased a book that has the potential to change your life for the better. Relationships are a significant part of our lives, and the quality of our relationships can often be in direct correlation with the quality of our lives. By using the information in this book, you will be able to improve your relationships with others, most specifically with your romantic partner.

In this book, you will learn the origin and history of the Enneagram, and an in depth overview of its nine different personality types (also known as enneatypes). However, using the word "personality" may be doing a slight injustice to describing the Enneagram, because it is in actuality an all-encompassing classification of different types of people and goes beyond surface level archetypes, and explores and explains people's motivations and unconscious factors at work that motivate their behavior.

By understanding these ideas, you can become a better you by focusing on amplifying your positive traits, and diminishing and improving upon your negative traits. You will also be able to improve your relationship (even if the other person does not want to change) by being able to better understand why your partner acts in certain ways based on their enneatype—an understanding that can inform and improve the way you relate to your partner. People truly want to feel understood, and when they do, you can increase intimacy, trust, and satisfaction in your relationship. You will also be able to better manage, minimize, and work through conflict.

Here is an overview of what you can expect from each chapter:

Chapter 1

You will gain a deeper understanding of the Enneagram diagram, its history, and how the types can influence each other.

Chapters 2 – 3

You will learn how to identify what Enneagram type you are and the most likely type for your partner.

Chapter 4

Chapter 4 is broken down into an overview of each Enneagram type. Each type section includes a section on the type's stress point, the security point, and levels of development. It also includes information on how each type acts in a relationship as well as tips on how to improve your personal level of development. There are also tips on how to relate to your partner based on the tendencies of that type.

Chapter 5

This section describes every enneatype pairing, and discusses positive and negative traits of the relationship. Chapter 5 relationship pairing definitions are in order from Type 1 to Type 9. If you're one of the higher number types such as Type 8 or Type 9, you will have to refer to your partner's lower number type. This is to prevent repeat information.

Chapter 6

Finally, a discussion guide is included to help you communicate and connect with your partner and apply the things you've learned to the betterment of your relationship.

Note: The pronoun "they" will be used throughout the book to mean "he or she" in the context of referring to one's partner.

Chapter 1:

What Is The Enneagram And What Are The Enneagram Personality Types?

What is the Enneagram?

Enneagram (pronounced any-a-gram) in Greek means nine-pointed line drawing. The Enneagram structure is a clocklike structure with 9 points, with each of the points representing a different personality type. The nine points are connected in a specific way to show how each Enneagram type can adapt traits from two other connected types depending on life's circumstances.

Nine is in the 12 o'clock position of the Enneagram structure, with Type One to the right. From Type One, you can count in a clockwise rotation around the circle until you arrive back at Type Nine on the top.

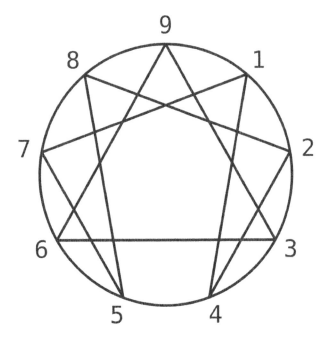

The Enneagram Structure

History of the Enneagram

The Enneagram's existence can be traced back as far as the 4th century, but despite its ancient origins, the specific personality types we refer to as enneatypes today have been introduced and studied (at the time of this writing) within the last 75 years, and several key figures have played a role in the recent evolution of the Enneagram and its rise to prominence in society.

George I. Gurdjieff

George Gurdjieff, a mystic, spiritual teacher, and philosopher, used the structure in the early 20th century to represent movement in dance training. Along with music, speeches, and his writings, dance and body movement were one of many tools he used in his spiritual teachings. Gurdjieff referenced the Enneagram's three centers to recognize similarities and differences between people. However, he is not considered the father of the Enneagram types as we know them today.

Oscar Ichazo

As a philosopher, Oscar Ichazo dedicated his life to gathering knowledge on inner work, leading him to create the Arica School in Chile to pass on his knowledge of self-realization to willing pupils as interested as he was in the fields of spirituality and psychology. During the 1950s – 1960s, he linked ego-types to the nine points on the Enneagram figure, thus forming the "Enneagram of Personality," sometimes referred to as "Enneagon" within the context of his teachings.

Claudio Naranjo

Claudio Naranjo was a psychiatrist who studied under Ichazo at his Arica School. After learning of the Enneagram of Personality from Ichazo, to Ichazo's dismay, Naranjo developed his own interpretations, and helped connect Ichazo's ego-types to DSM* personality definitions, thus forming the modern Enneagram that is most utilized today. In 1970, Claudio Naranjo became the psychological father of the Enneagram personality types as we now know them.

*DSM refers to the Diagnostic and Statistical Manual for Personality Disorders.

The Enneagram Structure

A Detailed Map Of The Three Centers And Their Types

The Enneagram structure is divided into three sections: The Gut (instinct driven), The Heart (emotionally driven), and The Head (intellect driven). Enneagram Types 1, 8, and 9 belong to the Gut group. Enneagram Types 2, 3, and 4 belong to the Heart group. Enneagram Types 5, 6, and 7 belong to the Head group.

The Gut (also called The Body) group of personalities are referred to as The Challenger (Type 8), The Peacemaker (Type 9), and The Reformer (Type 1). These types are driven by action.

The Heart group of personalities are referred to as The Helper (Type 2), The Achiever (Type 3), and The Individualist (Type 4). These types are driven by feeling.

The Head group of personalities include The Investigator (Type 5), The Loyalist (Type 6), and The Enthusiast (Type 7). These types are driven by thinking.

Each Enneagram type further breaks down into two additional tendencies known as a wing type. Wing types are based on neighboring types. For example, Type 9 core personality types can sometimes demonstrate traits of a Type 8 or Type 1. Also, stress and growth points can affect a person's personality traits.

These stress and growth points are indicated by the straight lines that stretch across the Enneagram figure. Using Type 9 as an example again, the stress and growth types are Type 6 and Type 3. Depending on the situation, an enneatype may demonstrate negative traits of their stress point type, or positive traits of their growth point type. The line of stretch is also known as the line of stress, and the line of growth is also known as the line of release or security.

The Power of the Number Three

The number three has been quite significant to humans throughout history. A complete thought or process is comprised of a beginning, middle, and end. In writing, we have our introduction, body, and conclusion. Many religions recognize three higher powers, such as the trinity in Christianity. When we think of the wholeness of health, we consider our body, our head, and our heart.

The Enneagram only further enforces the idea of the power of the number three. Nine is the square of three, or 3 x 3. Each personality type represented by the Enneagram is also influenced by three parts: the wing personality, the stress point of a personality type, and the growth point of a personality type. Each of the three points is located within each of the three centers powered by the head, heart, or body.

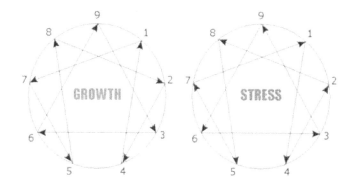

Diagram Of The Movement Between Each Enneagram Type And Its Lines Of Stress And Growth.

Stress Points

- Type 1 displays the negative traits of Type 4 during times of stress.
- Type 2 displays the negative traits of Type 8 during times of stress.
- Type 3 displays the negative traits of Type 9 during times of stress.
- Type 4 displays the negative traits of Type 2 during times of stress.
- Type 5 displays the negative traits of Type 7 during times of stress.
- Type 6 displays the negative traits of Type 3 during times of stress.
- Type 7 displays the negative traits of Type 1 during times of stress.

- Type 8 displays the negative traits of Type 5 during times of stress.
- Type 9 displays the negative traits of Type 6 during times of stress.

Security Points

- Type 1 displays the positive traits of Type 7 during times of growth.
- Type 2 displays the positive traits of Type 4 during times of growth.
- Type 3 displays the positive traits of Type 6 during times of growth.
- Type 4 displays the positive traits of Type 1 during times of growth.
- Type 5 displays the positive traits of Type 8 during times of growth.
- Type 6 displays the positive traits of Type 9 during times of growth.
- Type 7 displays the positive traits of Type 5 during times of growth.
- Type 8 displays the positive traits of Type 2 during times of growth.
- Type 9 displays the positive traits of Type 3 during times of growth.

Levels of Development

There are nine levels of development for each Enneagram type. Levels one, two, and three are the healthiest, highest-functioning levels of that particular type. Levels four, five, and six are average levels of development. Levels seven, eight, and nine are unhealthy levels of development. Many times, people in levels eight and nine may need professional help to achieve a healthy level for their type. By increasing your stage of development, you will be able to experience a healthier relationship.

Chapter 4 will give you tips you can focus on to improve towards a healthy stage of development.

Philosophy Behind the Enneagram

The foundation of the Enneagram structure and personality types is based on spiritual and ancient Greek philosophies. It is based on the fundamental beliefs that there is good and bad in everyone. It is also based on the belief that one type would not be complete without qualities of at least three other types. Some people, including Claudio Naranjo, believe everyone exhibits features from each personality type. Others believe people go through different types as they develop through life.

For example, your primary type before age 25 may not be your primary type in your 40s. The purpose of the Enneagram personality types is not to just tell you, "This is why you act the way you do, accept it."

Instead, it helps you understand yourself and your type better, so you can adapt to your strengths and weaknesses, and use your weaknesses as an impetus for intentional growth. The Enneagram will give you a foundation to work on improving yourself, know how to overcome your weaknesses, and cope with others as you manage their weaknesses.

Like what you see so far?

Please **leave a review on Amazon**

letting us know!

Chapter 2:

What Is Your Enneagram Type?

There are a few ways you can use this book to determine your most prominent Enneagram type.

First, thoroughly read through each type listed. There can be overlapping traits between the types. Read through the levels of development listed for each type. By understanding how stress and security points interact with each type, you may be able to point back to your core type.

Additionally, read the type pairings. Sometimes, it can be easier to see someone else's type rather than your own. By reading the type pairings, your personal enneatype should become clearer as you see how your type interacts with others.

Finally, if you have narrowed down your possible Enneagram type, you may decide to ask your partner or other people close to you what traits they feel describe you (good and bad). Sometimes we can be blind to traits other people can clearly see in us. (The discussion guide in Chapter 6 can be a good place to start learning how someone else sees you.)

While there are tests you can take online to help determine your type, taking personality tests can confuse people more than help. People usually change their answers on personality tests depending on their current situations.

This could end up pointing you toward a stress or security point depending on your current mood and circumstances instead of pointing you towards your core type. People also subconsciously tend to answer questions based on how they want to see themselves versus how they actually are.

For these reasons, I recommend that you pinpoint your type by studying the material in this book. It is comprehensive enough to enlighten you to your enneatype, and in studying all the types, you will have learned enough information to figure out how to best relate with all the types.

Chapter 3:

What Is Your Partner's Enneagram Type?

So, you think you know your partner? Do you think your partner knows you?

The definitions in this book will give you an understanding of the nine Enneagram personality types, and help you determine which one best suits your partner. However, don't forget that there can be different expressions of each type. Keep in mind the same information you had to be mindful of when determining your own type. Don't mistake an expression of a wing type, security point, or stress point as your partner's core enneatype.

Just as a personality test can only reveal our current state, a temporary emotional state or expression of your partner does not necessarily determine their core enneatype. Also keep in mind that your partner may have qualities and traits you are not completely aware of. You may pinpoint them as a particular type, yet after digging deeper into the information in this book, your partner may identify themselves as a different type than the one you had in mind.

This is one of many great uses of the discussion guide in Chapter 6. You can walk through it together with your partner, sharing your feelings and observations about yourselves and each other. By asking additional questions and getting each other's opinions on your respective enneatypes, you will gain a deeper understanding of one another. Most importantly, listen to your partner without being judgmental.

This book shares the good, the bad, and the ugly about each and every type. With that in mind, it can be easy to focus on your own positive traits and your partner's negative traits. Instead of being quick to point fingers to your partner's negative traits, be willing to learn why your partner has those traits. Negative traits can be a sign of stress.

Also pay attention to your partner's possible wing, stress, and security points. Use all of this information in a way that helps your partner and your relationship. It is intended to help you understand one another on a deeper level and gain insight into each other's fears, desires, and motivations, so you can better relate to one another. By reading the section on type pairings, you may also gain an understanding of how your partner sees you and how they interpret your actions.

Chapter 4:

The Enneagram Types

Type One

"The Reformer"

(Gut Center)

Reformers have a mission to change the world! They are always coming up with the best ways to overcome hardships. They always justify the reasoning for their missions and feel compelled to do anything they can to improve the world around them.

Ones are meticulous and ethical. They know what is right and acceptable and expect the same from others. Teaching is a common career choice for Ones. They also spend their time as activists, advocating for change. They strive to avoid making mistakes.

Ones are well organized and orderly and can become demanding of the people around them. Their high standards can cause them to be too critical of others, and they can come off as perfectionists.

High level One personalities are most likely to abandon their own comfortable lifestyles for the betterment of others. They will do extraordinary things to improve the quality of life for others.

Lower level Ones need to learn to separate their self-worth from their performance when they make mistakes. Instead of beating themselves up about their mishaps, they should use them as opportunities to learn.

If you are a Type One, by accepting that you are not expected to be perfect all the time, you can use your inner voice for growth instead of criticism. Lower level Ones may also have a problem with seeing the fault in themselves, but have no problem seeing faults in others.

Type One with a Nine-Wing tends to be more idealistic and want things reformed to their way, while Type One with a Two-Wing has a desire to help people, and they can become advocates or missionaries in their own right.

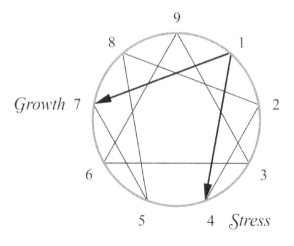

Stress And Growth Points For Type 1

Stress Point

Ones are likely to demonstrate unhealthy traits of the Type Four personality when under stress.

These traits include:

- Depression
- Narcissism
- Feelings of despair and hopelessness
- Shame
- Avoidance

Growth Point

Ones are likely to demonstrate average to healthy level traits or feelings associated with the Type Seven personality during times of growth.

These include:

- Joy
- Appreciation
- Enthusiasm
- Goodness of Life
- Gratitude
- Extroversion
- Productivity
- Practicality

Levels of Development

Each number in this section represents a level of development for the core type being discussed in this section (Type One). The levels are continuous in that levels one, two, and three are healthy levels of the type, while levels four, five, and six are average, and seven, eight, and nine are unhealthy levels of the particular type. The levels of development can help pinpoint the different variations in the continuum of expression of the core type, and can help pinpoint areas for growth for that particular type.

Healthy:

LEVEL ONE

Extraordinary discernment and wisdom – They understand the most realistic course of action to solve problems.

LEVEL TWO

Reliable personal convictions – Level two Ones' sense of right and wrong aligns with their religious and moral values. They desire to be reasonable, rational, and self-disciplined, and they want to achieve balance and maturity in all things.

LEVEL THREE

High principles – Level three Ones strive to be ethical, fair, and objective. Justice and truth are their primary values. Their sense of purpose, responsibility, and integrity help them teach others and maintain an eye and respect for the truth.

Average:

LEVEL FOUR

Idealist critics, crusaders, and advocates – Level four Ones are not satisfied with reality. It becomes their personal mission to improve everything. These are the people constantly serving multiple causes. They have a strong sense of how they feel things should be.

LEVEL FIVE

Afraid of making mistakes – Everything must be consistent with their ideals. Level five Ones are well-organized but impersonal and emotionally distant. They do not let their feelings or impulses control their actions in any way. They are workaholics, punctual, and demanding.

LEVEL SIX

Judgmental perfectionists – Level six Ones are very opinionated about everything, causing them to be highly critical of themselves and those around them. They constantly scold people who will never be able to live up to their standards of perfection. They can come across as abrasive and angry.

Unhealthy:

LEVEL SEVEN

Dogmatic – Level seven Ones are inflexible, intolerant, and self-righteous. They believe they are the only ones who can be right. They are strict in judgment but rationalize their own actions.

LEVEL EIGHT

Hypocritical – Level eight Ones obsess over the imperfections and mistakes of others, but they are blind to their own actions.

LEVEL NINE

Severely depressed and obsessive – Level nine Ones push others away to separate themselves from the imperfections of others. They may experience severe depression or nervous breakdowns. Obsessive-compulsive disorder and depressive personality disorders are common mental health issues suffered by Ones at this level.

How to Improve Your Current Stage of Development

Understand that it is okay to make mistakes and be wrong sometimes. Realize you need to make mistakes in order to learn and improve from them.

Have compassion for yourself. (Even when you make a mistake)

Recognize when you are being too critical of yourself and others.

Make time to have fun, relax, and accept who you are.

Learn to appreciate the small things in life.

In Relationships (For Your Partner's Understanding)

Ones pay close attention to the small details. You can help your partner by trying to remember important details like dates and care instructions.

Show high respect for your partner by asking for permission and considering your partner's opinions and feelings.

Compliment your partner on specific qualities and achievements.

Continually improve your own character without bragging about your achievements. To Type One personalities, improving your character should be a given without a need for acknowledgment.

Always be upfront and honest about your own mistakes. Do not try to hide wrongdoings from your partner.

Help your partner learn how to have fun and enjoy life.

Use tasteful humor to help ease your partner's worries.

Agree to disagree. Ones need to be right, so try to incorporate your partner's methods while also showing your partner more than one method can work.

Type Ones tend to spend many hours alone so it can be helpful to have your own interests and hobbies.

Type Two

"The Helper"

(Heart Center)

Type Two personalities are considered helpers because they are warm-hearted and empathetic. Their goal is to help people and serve others, even though that can mean sometimes neglecting their own needs. While Type Twos genuinely try their best to help others whenever they can, they also love to be recognized as being helpful. They feel sharing love and concern for others is the best way to live. Family and friendship are especially important to Type Two personalities.

Type Twos are compassionate and understanding. They have seemingly unlimited patience and are always willing to help others. Twos are well-meaning, but sometimes their drive to help others becomes a need to be needed. They often have problems recognizing and admitting their own needs. People are drawn to Type Twos and many times take advantage of their generosity.

A healthy Two will know how and when to let go of people in their life, while unhealthier Type Twos have a hard time letting go and insist on being needed. Unhealthy Twos validate their self-worth by how much of themselves they sacrifice for others. They trade generosity and over-involvement to obtain the love they secretly desire. Their basic desire to feel loved leads to a central fear of being unwanted or feeling unworthy of love.

Personal development may be hindered by a tendency to become over-involved in the lives of those around them. Twos feel they are nothing without their great acts of service. Self-development requires visiting dark places in our subconscious – a place Type Twos avoid. They prefer to see themselves as completely positive and full of light.

Type Twos with a One-Wing may fall into the role of a servant. They direct their need to be needed to serving others, many times to a fault. Type Twos with a Three-Wing may serve the role of a host/hostess so to speak. They enjoy being able to bring people closer together.

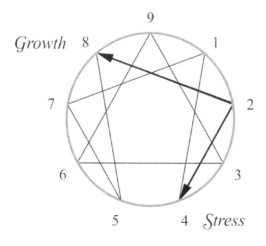

Stress And Growth Points For Type 2

Stress Point

Twos are likely to demonstrate the unhealthy level traits of the Type Eight personality when under stress.

These traits can manifest as being:

- Vengeful
- Callous
- Hard-hearted
- Antisocial
- Totalitarian
- Reckless
- Confrontational
- Threatening
- Proud

- Domineering
- Self-sufficient
- Dictatorial
- Immoral
- Violent
- Murderous
- Sociopathic
- Feeling invincible

Growth Point

Twos are likely to demonstrate the average to healthy level traits of the Type Four personality during times of growth.

These traits can manifest as being:

- Creative
- Inspired
- Self-aware
- Sensitive to others
- Gentle
- Tactful
- Compassionate
- Individualistic
- Humane

Levels of Development

Healthy:

LEVEL ONE

Humble – Healthy level Twos are unselfish and altruistic. They have unconditional love to offer others. They consider it a privilege to be involved in the lives of others.

LEVEL TWO

Compassionate – Type Twos in this stage of development have sincere empathy for the feelings of others. They truly care about other people's needs. They are warm-hearted, thoughtful, and forgiving.

LEVEL THREE

Encouraging – Level three Twos see the good in others. They are healthy enough to remember to take care of themselves as well as others. Twos are nurturing and generous in their giving – truly loving.

Average:

LEVEL FOUR

People-pleasers – Level four Twos may try to show off their loving nature and attempt to become too close to people.

LEVEL FIVE

Overly intrusive – Level five Twos need to be needed. They try to meddle and control the lives of others in the name of love. They start to become codependent and self-sacrificial. Twos believe they can never do enough for others.

LEVEL SIX

Overbearing – Level six Twos become a "martyr" for others. They tend to overrate the impact of their efforts for the benefit of others. They believe they are indispensable, and other people need them. At times, they may be patronizing and presumptuous.

Unhealthy:

LEVEL SEVEN

Manipulative – Level seven Twos are self-serving. They tell people how much the other person "owes" them. At this stage, they are likely to abuse food or drugs to "stuff their feelings" and get sympathy from the people around them. They may make belittling remarks to undermine people. Twos are self-deceptive about how damaging their behavior and motives are.

LEVEL EIGHT

Coercive – Level eight Twos may become domineering. They feel they are entitled to repayment for all the service they gave to others.

LEVEL NINE

Victims – Unhealthy level Twos rationalize their behavior by becoming victims. They are angry and resentful towards others. Many people in this stage can become hypochondriacs. They use health problems, real or imagined, to get attention.

How to Improve Your Current Stage of Development

Be open to your own needs and wants. Take time to ask yourself what you need.

Pay attention to your health. Many times, health problems occur from personal neglect.

Understand how avoiding personal needs can affect your relationships. You can't help others when you neglect yourself.

Choose a partner who will appreciate your care and your giving, and not take advantage of you.

Make quality time for yourself without media or interference.

Learn to become independent by putting some of your own needs first.

In Relationships (For Your Partner's Understanding)

Twos are more likely to have emotional issues and anxiety when their needs are not met.

They are likely to create problems to solve. They want to be helpful to their partner and may try to solve "problems" you may not see as problems.

Twos believe you do not love them if you do not meet their needs.

Your Type Two partner may not shower you with attention because they are upset and withdrawing from you as a consequence, or because other people's needs appear to be more urgent at the moment.

There may be times when you need to gently remind your partner you can take care of your own needs.

Encourage your partner to make time for themselves.

Type Three

"The Achiever"

(Heart Center)

Achievers are success-oriented and practical. They are driven, and adapt to situations as needed so they can excel in everything they do. Threes are concerned with how people perceive them. They want others to see them as competent, and able to get the job done. They want to make every aspect of their life a success and a model for others.

Type Threes have a charming sense of energy. They are poised, diplomatic, self-assured, and ambitious. They are highly driven for advancement in their positions. Healthy Threes are more than capable of achieving great things to change the world.

People look up to them because of their accomplishments and their graciousness. They enjoy motivating others to work hard and see how much they too can accomplish. Healthy Threes feel good developing their abilities, and contributing those abilities to people around them.

These are your typical workaholics and competitors. To other people, threes may be considered the "teacher's pet" or a "brown-noser." They can be seen going out of their way to stay late at work and skipping breaks to get a job done. Type Threes work extremely well under pressure.

Threes' basic desire to feel worthwhile and valuable can instill a fear of being worthless. They may become consumed with other people's definition of success. This can cause them to lose sight of who they really are, due to their pursuit of success for other people rather than personal gain.

Type Threes perceive emotions as a roadblock to success. Being in tune with their own desires might make them lose respect from others. Therefore, they box up their feelings and interests to appear successful.

This need to drown their feelings is usually fueled by how they were raised. They might have been pressured to believe they were worthless unless they excelled in certain areas. Many people receive the same type of message, but Threes really take it to heart the most. When confronted with the question, "What do I personally want from life?" They generally do not have an answer because they were never allowed to explore their own interests.

Threes with a Two-Wing may be classified as a charmer, while Threes with a Four-Wing are classified as a professional.

Type Threes have a strong need for affirmation and rewards. They expect an acknowledgment of their achievements and may feel used and undervalued when they are not acknowledged for their work.

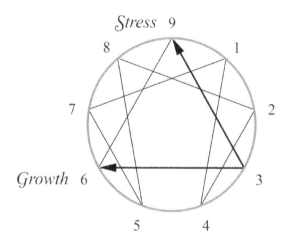

Stress And Growth Points For Type 3

Stress Point

Threes are likely to demonstrate unhealthy level traits of the Type Nine personality during times of stress.

These traits include being:

- Withdrawn
- Numb
- Stubborn
- Neglectful
- Desiring of "peace at any cost"
- Guilty of tuning out reality
- Apt to idealize others

Growth Point

Threes are likely to demonstrate average to healthy level traits of the Type Six personality during times of growth.

These traits include being:

- Independent
- Cooperative
- Endearing
- Responsible
- Hard-working
- Persevering

Levels of Development

Healthy:

LEVEL ONE

Self-accepting – Level one Threes are authentically modest, charitable, gentle, and benevolent. They are full of heart, and they humor others by jokingly putting themselves down.

LEVEL TWO

Self-assured – Level two Threes have high self-esteem and know how competent they are. They have confidence in their self-worth. They are charming and gracious. They adapt well to any situation.

LEVEL THREE

Ambitious – This level of Threes make outstanding role models, and others become motivated to mirror them in positive ways. They will do anything to improve themselves into becoming their "best self."

Average:

LEVEL FOUR

High performing – Level four threes are terrified of failing. They strive for excellence and success. Their self-worth diminishes if they are not the best.

LEVEL FIVE

Image-conscious – Level five Threes are fully concerned with their reputation and how others perceive them. They begin to lose touch with their feelings and ideas.

LEVEL SIX

Narcissistic – Level six Threes may exaggerate their accomplishments and embellish their strengths. They become arrogant in their attempt to seek attention and acknowledgment.

Unhealthy:

LEVEL SEVEN

Manipulative – Level seven Threes envy the success of others and are willing to fudge ethics to gain an edge. They may lie and cheat to gain promotions.

LEVEL EIGHT

Devious – Level eight Threes will become malicious towards others. They attempt to sabotage other people's chance of success.

LEVEL NINE

Vindictive – Unhealthy Threes at this level are relentless in ruining others' happiness. They become obsessed with destroying evidence of their failures.

How to Improve Your Current Stage of Development

Take time to slow down and "smell the roses."

Go for a slow walk in the park to help you unwind and become more mindful.

Be aware of your emotions, even negative ones.

Understand success is not immediate. It takes failure to create success.

Learn to separate a person's worth from their medals and achievements. This goes for you as well.

Learn to love and forgive yourself.

Let your partner love you for being you. On that same note, love your partner for their true self and not their achievements.

Learn to fully listen to your partner without interrupting and jumping to conclusions.

In Relationships (For Your Partner's Understanding)

Threes can be known for subconsciously withholding information they feel puts themselves or people they care about in a negative light.

Threes have a hard time processing their emotions. Understand that your partner's true emotions may differ from they may think or act like their emotions are.

Your partner may seem like a busybody trying to fill their time with productive activities.

Use high energy outings to connect with your partner.

Sometimes you may have to remind your partner to slow down for quality time together.

Acknowledge your partner's achievements – even the small ones.

Type Four

"The Individualist"

(Heart Center)

Individualists are sensitive and introspective. They can be dramatic and expressive about the situations happening in their lives. They can also be self-absorbed and temperamental.

Fours are very self-aware, which can make them feel self-conscious about their faults. They dwell on the characteristics that make them defective, and also dwell on what they can do to create an identity separate from those around them. They typically have a negative self-image and low self-esteem. While they tend to be emotionally honest, their self-consciousness can also make them more reserved. They may withdraw from others when they become vulnerable and feel defective.

They want to be extraordinary, and have great disdain for living ordinary lifestyles. This causes them to have problems with their self-worth when melancholy and self-indulgence creep in, developing a sense of self-pity.

On a positive note, Fours are highly creative and inspired. They use their creativity to transform experiences. They use inspiration to renew their spirits. Fours' true desire is to find their identity and discover every aspect of their personality. Fours typically feel as if they are lacking, but they usually can't pinpoint exactly what they feel they are lacking in.

Their biggest fear is not being able to leave behind a significant legacy for others to remember them by.
They want to appear as an individualist that can stand out in a crowd. In a relationship, they desire someone who will appreciate the identity they have created. Fours need someone who sees them as unique and appreciates their uniqueness even more than they do.

Healthy Fours can own up to their feelings and appreciate the little things that make them unique. They are not ashamed of their setbacks and weaknesses. They would rather embrace their identity even if they do not like what they see.

Lower level Fours may create a "Fantasy Self-Image" of who they want to be. In their mind, they may embellish their skills and abilities. However, when asked to perform these special skills, they become embarrassed because the truth does not match their fantasy.

The harshness they put on themselves allows them to endure painful experiences better than other types. Fours may hang on to their negativity until it starves them of happiness. They will not recognize their treasures until they stop putting themselves down and start living up to positive affirmations.

Fours with a Three-Wing are more aristocratic. On the other hand, Fours with a Five-Wing have a bohemian attitude.

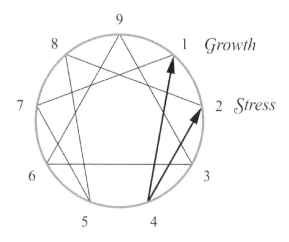

Stress And Growth Points For Type 4

Stress Point

Fours are likely to demonstrate unhealthy traits of the Type Two personality during times of stress.

These traits include being:

- Intrusive
- Presumptuous
- Manipulative
- Domineering
- Victimized
- People-pleaser

Growth Point

Fours are likely to demonstrate average to healthy traits of the Type One personality during times of growth.

These traits include being:

- Wise
- Discerning
- Conscientious
- Principled
- Responsible
- Ethical

Levels of Development

Healthy:

LEVEL ONE

Creative – Healthy Fours express themselves and their perceived universe through art. They transform their situations into valuable learning experiences.

LEVEL TWO

Introspective – Level two Fours are aware of their personal feelings and attributes. They can be sensitive to themselves. Towards others, they are tactful, gentle, and compassionate.

LEVEL THREE

Emotionally aware – Level three Fours reveal their emotions honestly. They have an ironic view on life. They can be both serious and funny. Fours in this stage may be both emotionally strong, but also vulnerable.

Average:

LEVEL FOUR

Imaginative – Fours at this level use their fantasies to beautify their lives.

LEVEL FIVE

Hypersensitive – Level five Fours may become too in touch with their feelings. They take everything personally. They are likely to become introverted and self-conscious.

LEVEL SIX

Self-pity – Level six Fours are impractical in their view of their lifestyle. They feel they are exempt from living like an "ordinary" person. They envy those with more exciting lifestyles, becoming self-indulgent to their wants.

Unhealthy:

LEVEL SEVEN

Ashamed – Level seven Fours are ashamed of themselves when their plans fail. They get depressed and alienate from the world, so they don't have to see what they could have been.

LEVEL EIGHT

Contempt – Level eight Fours are surrounded by a personal hell, being tormented by their thoughts. They blame others around them for their failure and drive away anyone who may try to help.

LEVEL NINE

Despair – Unhealthy Fours are prone to emotional breakdowns. They begin to feel hopeless, finding addictions to help them escape their personal torment.

How to Improve Your Current Stage of Development

Stay focused on the positive aspects of your life.

Work consistently toward your goals, even if your emotions tell you that you don't feel like it.

Learn to accept that your feelings do not determine reality.

Instead of constantly flipping the focus of a conversation on yourself, learn to listen to your partner and their needs.

Count your small blessings. Find little things each day to appreciate and be grateful for.

Utilize physical exercise to release your emotions. Walking, running, and yoga can be very beneficial to your mental and emotional health.

Step out from the crowd at work and social events. This will help you keep your self-consciousness in check.

In Relationships (For Your Partner's Understanding)

Fours are prone to frequent mood swings unrelated to your actions. Don't take this personally.

Give your partner space, but let them know you are still there for them.

You can help reassure your partner by staying calm in stressful situations.

Fours may try to push you away, yet complain when you become distant.

Fours appreciate stimulation by keeping things fun and random. They like spontaneity and are bored by predictability.

Type Five

"The Investigator"

(Head Center)

Investigators are intense and intellectual. They are insightful, curious, perceptive, and alert. Fives are innovative and inventive, but they prefer to be independent, which can also make them secretive and isolated. They tend to get lost in their minds, contemplating solutions. They enjoy solving mental puzzles.

Many times, they focus too much energy on academic knowledge. They neglect developing social and practical skills. They can become detached from society, causing them to develop problems with nihilism, eccentricity, and isolation.

In a positive light, Fives are visionary pioneers. They are considered "ahead of their time" because they see the world and situations they encounter in a unique way that is not evident to others. Fives are not turned on by the tried and true. Instead, they want to be the ones to discover uncharted territory, and want to be the first to know something. Fives are motivated to learn as much as they can about the world around them. Many Fives will find one special niche they feel they can master.

They plan everything and use knowledge to protect themselves from setbacks. Fives fear being useless, so they develop their mental capacity to devise enlightening solutions to complicated problems. They do not necessarily believe they have unique skills to offer. They instead use their research abilities to learn new skills, so they have something to contribute to the world. They may use their knowledge and observations to invent something useful. Their contributions make them feel valued as a person, but they want to be careful to wait until they know it works.

Fives are considered investigators because they strive to explore and learn as much as they can about how and why things are the way they are. They even investigate their own feelings and imaginations. However, they are also the world's toughest skeptics. They question everyone's theories until they are confident in their beliefs, so they can explain as much as they can about the inner workings of life.

Type Fives with a Four-Wing may be considered eccentric, while Type Fives with a Six-Wing are problem solvers.

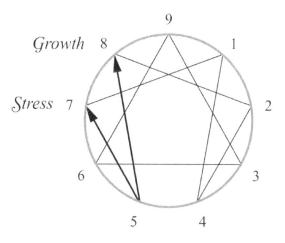

Stress And Growth Points For Type 5

Stress Point

Fives are likely to demonstrate unhealthy traits of the Type Seven personality during times of stress.

This includes being:

- Uninhibited
- Impulsive
- "Overly" Adventurous
- Demanding
- Bipolar

- Having erratic mood swings

Growth Point

Fives are likely to demonstrate average to healthy traits of the Type Eight personality during times of growth.

These traits include being:

- Self-restrained
- Merciful
- Resourceful
- Decisive
- Authoritative
- Self-confident
- Self-sufficient

Levels of Development

Healthy:

LEVEL ONE

Visionary – Healthy Fives are open-minded and make pioneering discoveries. Their capacity for new knowledge is limitless.

LEVEL TWO

Observant – Level two Fives are mentally alert and focused. Their curiosity leads them to more knowledge.

LEVEL THREE

Knowledge Master – Level three Fives study their chosen field until they become "master of their domain."

Average:

LEVEL FOUR

Studious – Level four Fives obsess over making sure all their theories are accurate and fit together. Blueprints and models fill their office, either literally or figuratively.

LEVEL FIVE

Detached – Fives in this stage preoccupy themselves with off-beat subjects that do not pertain to the practical world.

LEVEL SIX

Antagonistic – Level six Fives are cynical and abrasive toward anyone who does not accept their views.

Unhealthy:

LEVEL SEVEN

Reclusive – Level seven Fives fear aggression and rejection of their ideas, so they avoid social engagements.

LEVEL EIGHT

Phobic – Unhealthy Fives obsess over the dangers of the world and develop crazy phobias. Even if there is only a one in a million chance of danger, they will fear it.

LEVEL NINE

Schizophrenic – By this point, Fives have had a devastating break from reality. They become deranged by their imaginations and abhor the truth.

How to Improve Your Current Stage of Development

Let yourself experience feelings, even when others are around.

Learn to discern who you can trust. Be willing to share your personal experiences and feelings with your partner. Start by sharing one detail you would not share normally.

Learn how other people communicate emotions non-verbally, such as body language, tone, or speech style.

Begin high energy physical activity to stay grounded.

In Relationships (For Your Partner's Understanding)

Use a shared interest to get your partner to open up in conversation.

Fives are likely to keep their friendships and interests separate from their romantic relationship.

Fives have strong feelings even when they do not show it.

Your partner is more likely to stay calm and objective in stressful situations. However, they are also more likely to step up their game to get things done rather than reach out for help.

Too many expectations put a burden on your partner to try to live up to. They can be more stressed and overwhelmed by this than other types.

Pay attention to small, non-verbal gestures such as a gift or service.

Type Six

"The Loyalist"

(Head Center)

Loyalists are committed to others and focused on safety and security. They are hard-working, reliable, trustworthy, and responsible. They anticipate problems and react quickly to help solve them.

But at times, they become too cautious, resulting in indecisiveness. Sixes are too involved in their thoughts and the what-ifs to have confidence in their decisions. They begin to worry about what could happen. Most of the time, the scenarios in their minds are much worse than the reality of what is most likely to actually happen.

Healthy Sixes can be engaging and responsible. Lower functioning Sixes become anxious and suspicious. When problems become more than they can handle and they become anxious, they combat that anxiety by being defensive and evasive. Sixes struggle with suspicion and self-doubt. Their self-doubt stems from their lack of confidence in themselves. They need support and guidance from others to feel secure in their choices.

Sixes are loyal to a fault. They hang on to relationships for better or for worse, many times unfortunately for the worse. They stick around for the long-haul even when the relationship is strained and even when they personally suffer. They will fight for their beliefs, their family, and their community more than their own personal needs.

At the same time, many Sixes can go with the flow and be loyal to others' beliefs and ideas, while some Sixes may try to step out and be revolutionary or even rebellious. Sixes can be defined by their contradictory manner, making them more difficult to understand.

Depending on their situation, Sixes can be:

- Strong and weak
- Trusting and distrusting
- Fearful and courageous
- Defenders and provokers
- Sweet and sour
- Bully and weak
- Aggressive and passive
- Defensive and offensive
- Social and loner

- Believers and doubters
- Tender and mean
- Cooperative and obstructive
- Generous and petty

Sixes must learn to face their anxieties and personal issues before they can become courageous and serene in any circumstance.

Sixes with a Five-Wing are defenders, while Sixes with a Seven-Wing are more like a buddy.

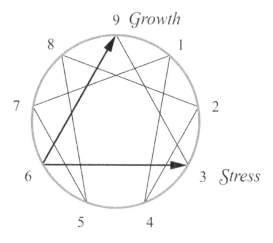

Stress And Growth Points For Type 6

Stress Point

Sixes are likely to demonstrate unhealthy traits of the Type Three personality during times of stress.

These traits include being:

- Image-conscious
- Narcissistic
- Manipulative
- Devious
- Vindictive

Growth Point

Sixes are likely to demonstrate average to unhealthy traits of the Type Nine personality during times of growth.

These traits include being:

- Independent
- Self-sufficient
- Patient
- Self-effacing
- Optimistic

Levels of Development

Healthy:

LEVEL ONE

Self-affirming – High functioning Sixes are confident in themselves, demonstrating courage and self-expression.

LEVEL TWO

Lovable – Level two Sixes gain emotional responses from others by appearing endearing and affectionate. They build trust that leads to permanent relationships and alliances.

LEVEL THREE

Dedicated – Level three Sixes work hard for the causes they believe in. Their partner can rely on Sixes to be there for them. Sixes create an environment of security and stability.

Average:

LEVEL FOUR

Vigilant – Level four Sixes lose trust in their own opinions and look to others for stable solutions. They are on alert for potential problems.

LEVEL FIVE

Passive-aggressive – Level five Sixes are evasive and indecisive in order to resist adding responsibilities to their plate. These Sixes also tend to be procrastinators.

LEVEL SIX

Sarcastic – To compensate for insecurities, Sixes in this stage blame others for their own problems. They become defensive and draw a hard line between friend and foe.

Unhealthy:

LEVEL SEVEN

Panic-stricken – When plans fail, and Sixes risk losing assets that make them feel secure, they start to panic and become volatile.

LEVEL EIGHT

Persecuted – Unhealthy level eight Sixes are paranoid and feel like life is out to get them. Many times, Sixes act out in a way that becomes a self-fulfilling prophecy – especially in relationships.

LEVEL NINE

Hysterical – Unhealthy Sixes at this level seek an escape route from the punishment of life. They may bring on self-inflicted injuries or contemplate suicide in severe cases. (**Please seek a professional if you or someone you know is in this stage.**)

How to Improve Your Current Stage of Development

Understand that everyone experiences insecurity in their life, and it is not something that is unique to you.

Have faith in yourself and in your partner. Build trust in others around you rather than always being skeptical and second-guessing a person's motives.

Keep your fears in check. Ask yourself about the likelihood of your worse fears being true. Many times, your worry is not warranted.

Do not let fear keep you from pursuing or achieving success.

In Relationships (For Your Partner's Understanding)

Uncertainty and doubt cause mood swings for Type Sixes.

Spontaneity and romance will reassure your partner of your love and commitment and help ease their insecurity in the relationship.

Denying problems in the relationship creates mistrust in your partner.

Sixes are likely to displace their own feelings onto you. For example, your partner may accuse you of being angry or withdrawn when it is really them feeling or behaving that way.

Be genuine when reassuring your partner.

Let your partner know you value them and their love for you.

Type Seven

"The Enthusiast"

(Head Center)

Enthusiasts are spontaneous and versatile. They are busy-bodies. However, they can also be acquisitive and scattered. They thrive on variety. Sevens are extroverted and optimistic. They are playful and high-spirited, but still practical. They are always seeking new, exciting experiences. Sevens are always scared they are going to "miss out" on having fun or be deprived of their basic needs. Sevens crave a comfortable and sometimes lavish lifestyle.

To many, they seem undisciplined because they seem to over-extend themselves to many interests. Some of these interests are not always well-matched with their true talents. While they seem to be scattered, many of their best ideas have been by impulse. Their "scattered" way of thinking helps them synthesize information and brainstorm ideas and solutions.

Their special abilities also equip them to learn new skills and absorb information more quickly than others. However, this is a double-edged sword because they are free to explore multiple interests and can be indecisive in their endeavors.

Sevens can be bold, pursuing life with curiosity and determination.

At their best, they put extraordinary focused energy into their goals. On a deeper level, you will find that Sevens share a common anxiety with Fives and Sixes. They fear they will not find satisfaction and comfort in life, which is why they bury this fear by pursuing multiple interests. They fear missing out if they do not try everything. The consequence of their incessant pursuits can be diminished health, strained relationships, and financial problems.

When Sevens are well-balanced, their joy and enthusiasm become contagious to those around them.

Sevens with a Six-Wing are entertainers, while Sevens with an Eight-Wing are realists.

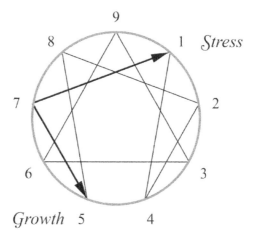

Stress And Growth Points For Type 7

Stress Point

Sevens are likely to demonstrate unhealthy traits of the Type One personality during times of stress.

These traits include being:

- Idealistic
- Puritanical
- Judgmental
- Perfectionistic
- Dogmatic
- Intolerant
- Hypocritical
- Advocative
- Punitive

Growth Point

Sevens are likely to demonstrate average to healthy traits of the Type Five personality during times of growth.

These traits include being:

- Skillful
- Independent
- Focused
- Curious
- Visionaries
- Observers

Levels of Development

Healthy:

LEVEL ONE

Full of life – Healthy Sevens seize the moment and enjoy life to the fullest. They enjoy the little things in life.

LEVEL TWO

Vivacious – Level two Sevens are extroverts. They are easily stimulated by small indulgences.

LEVEL THREE

Multi-talented – Level three Sevens are practical and productive. They enjoy developing many talents.

Average:

LEVEL FOUR

Adventurous – Level four Sevens need constant stimulation to stay focused. This level is adventurous. Sevens will seek out additional options and choices before planning a solution.

LEVEL FIVE

Hyperactive – Level five Sevens have a problem saying no to new responsibilities and opportunities. Instead, they throw themselves at many different adventures and are constantly active.

LEVEL SIX

Materialistic – Level six Sevens feel as if they never have enough. They are self-centered and always want more.

Unhealthy:

LEVEL SEVEN

Impulsive – Sevens in this stage do not know how to stop giving in to their addictions. They spread themselves thin with too many projects.

LEVEL EIGHT

Mania – Unhealthy Sevens have frequent mood swings and seem to be out of control.

LEVEL NINE

Bipolar – By this point, the Seven's health and energy are depleted. Sevens give up on themselves and life, succumbing to deep depression that can manifest itself as bipolar disorder.

How to Improve Your Current Stage of Development

Learn to take the bad with the good and learn from it.

Make small commitments you can stick to while building up to larger commitments.

Be mindful of focusing on just one project at a time. This will help you learn to finish the projects you start.

Have compassion toward your partner's feelings.

Learn to accept negative emotions rather than avoid them.

In Relationships (For Your Partner's Understanding)

There is no in between. Sevens will either love you or ignore you based on their current self-esteem.

They take criticism harshly and personally, so state the good before you critique the negative.

Sevens tend to be "preachy" when they are upset or stressed.

Sevens are always working and planning a grand scheme for their future.

Mutual creativity and happiness are important for a successful relationship.

Always be kind and thoughtful in dealings with your partner.

Type Eight

"The Challenger"

(Gut Center)

Challengers perceive themselves as powerful and dominating. Their self-confidence and decisiveness are expressed through confrontation. Type Eights are strong and assertive. They are protective and resourceful, but many times they express themselves by being ego-centric and domineering. Eights feel they must gain control of their environments, including the people around them. They do not let other people's opinions sway their actions.

On a positive note, Eights tend to have more willpower and vitality to push through challenges and achieve remarkable results. They also know how to challenge others so they can grow. In addition to their willpower, Eights also have incredible physical strength and can endure more physical pain than others. Healthy Eights can become masters of their strength and direct their power for good to help others.

However, they are terrified of emotional pain. They put on a façade of strength and power to protect their feelings and avoid rejection. They would rather reject others before they can be rejected. Eights struggle to keep their tempers in check. While they create a hardcore persona, deep down they struggle with becoming vulnerable.

Eights with a Seven-Wing are known as mavericks, while Eights with a Nine-Wing are known as the bear.

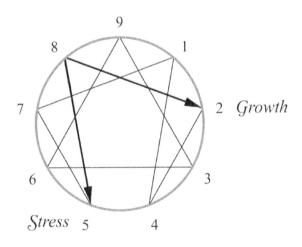

Stress And Growth Points For Type 8

Stress Point

Eights are likely to demonstrate unhealthy traits of the Type Five personality during times of stress.

These traits include being:

- Detached
- Antagonistic
- Reclusive
- Studious
- Delirious
- Schizophrenic

Growth Point

Eights are likely to demonstrate average to healthy traits of the Type Two personality during times of growth.

These traits include being:

- Humble
- Compassionate
- Appreciative
- Altruistic
- Empathetic
- Nurturing

Levels of Development

Healthy:

LEVEL ONE

Courageous – Healthy Eights achieve heroism and greatness by trading selfishness in favor of focusing on the greater good.

LEVEL TWO

Self-assertive – Level two Eights are confident in their abilities and their opinions. They have a can-do attitude and are reluctant to back down.

LEVEL THREE

Authoritative – Level three Eights take charge and make change happen. People look up to them and trust their judgments.

Average:

LEVEL FOUR

Self-sufficient – Level four Eights work hard and take risks to ensure their needs are met physically and financially.

LEVEL FIVE

Dominant – Level five Eights want to feel as if others support them, so they boss the people around them to accept their ideas.

LEVEL SIX

Combative – Level six Eights are confrontational to intimidate others into obedience.

Unhealthy:

LEVEL SEVEN

Dictatorial – Level seven Eights use their "might" to prove they are right. They use violence to get subordinates to obey them.

LEVEL EIGHT

Delusional – Unhealthy Eights at this level are delusional about how to get power and respect. They feel invincible as if nothing can bring them down.

LEVEL NINE

Vengeful – At the worst, Eights can be dangerous to be around because they attempt to destroy anything or anyone who does not conform to their will.

How to Improve Your Current Stage of Development

Learn that excessive force and brawn are not always necessary.

Consider how your brash behavior affects your partner.

Learn to allow yourself to be vulnerable, especially with your partner.

Learn to appreciate your partner's opinions and feelings. You do not always have to be right.

In Relationships (For Your Partner's Understanding)

Eights will test your strength, independence, and vitality.

While Eights can be very explosive, they quickly forget and move on once they feel the threat is over.

Usually, their expression of anger is a representation of their feeling of lack of connection in the relationship.

Eights live in an all or nothing world. They feel threatened by gray areas.

Be upfront about anything and everything with your Eight partner. They value direct contact. Even seemingly minor withheld information is considered a major betrayal.

Eights are power hungry. They make the rules, and they are the only one allowed to break them.

Despite their roughness, you can count on your partner to be there for you in the toughest times when no one else would be.

Type Nine

"The Peacemaker"

(Gut Center)

As the name suggests, Peacemakers are easygoing, agreeable, complacent, and reassuring. They can be creative and supportive to others. At their best, Nines are unshakable. They embrace the issues affecting those around them and help others work through their problems. Nines strive for peace, not only for others but also within themselves. They are most likely to seek guidance from the spiritual, or a higher power. The peace promised by religion appeals to their yearning for peace.

Nines may misidentify with the Intellectual (Five, Six, Seven) or Emotional (Two, Three, Four) because they do not trust their own instincts. Instead, they let their feelings sway their instincts and retreat to the depths of their minds to be comforted by mental fantasies.

They encapsulate the whole of the Enneagram types, therefore, lacking a true sense of identity.

Nines attempt to emphasize the positives in life and become numb when they can't find positive solutions. They tend to minimize problems, so they are not affected by them. Nines fear experiencing loss and separation. They believe if they can achieve peace, they will not be separated from others and other people will appreciate them. They need to learn how to cope with the negative and painful experiences of life.

Nines with an Eight-Wing are like a referee, while Nines with a One-Wing are dreamers.

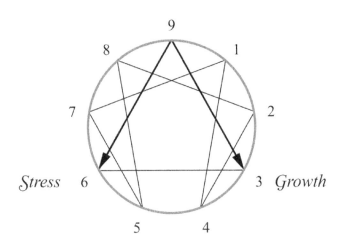

Stress And Growth Points For Type 9

Stress Point

Nines are likely to demonstrate unhealthy traits of the Type Six personality during times of stress.

These traits include being:

- Paranoid
- Panicky
- Hysterical
- Sarcastic
- Passive-Aggressive
- Evasive
- Procrastinating
- Feeling persecuted
- Feeling Defenseless
- Blaming other people
- Always anticipating problems
- Searching for security

Growth Point

Nines are likely to demonstrate average to healthy traits of the Type Three personality during times of growth.

These traits include being:

- Self-acceptant

- Energetic
- Ambitious
- Adaptable
- Benevolent

Levels of Development

Healthy:

LEVEL ONE

Content – Healthy Nines are in touch with themselves and others. They form deeper and more sincere relationships.

LEVEL TWO

Receptive – Level two Nines are emotionally strong. They easily trust others and are genuinely helpful and good-natured.

LEVEL THREE

Optimistic – Level three Nines easily bring people together and are optimistic about solving problems together.

Average:

LEVEL FOUR

Accommodating – Level four Nines idealize the people around them. They are quick to conform to others' wishes and say yes to things they do not want to do.

LEVEL FIVE

Complacent – Level five Nines are indifferent toward situations and disengage emotionally from problems. Instead, they try to act as if the problem is not even there.

LEVEL SIX

"Peace at any cost" – Level six Nines appease others and neglect their own needs. They can also become stubborn when they feel solutions are lacking. They procrastinate and may devise "creative" solutions that do not really work.

Unhealthy:

LEVEL SEVEN

Repressed – Level seven Nines lose confidence in their ability to solve problems. Therefore, they become neglectful of others and dissociate from conflict.

LEVEL EIGHT

Numb – Level eight Nines attempt to block out anything that may stir emotion.
They may show signs of Catatonia, Multiple Personality Disorder, Dissociative Identity Disorder, Schizophrenia, and Dependent Personality Disorder.

LEVEL NINE

Nines abandon their true self, and fully experience personality disorders like the ones mentioned above.

How to Improve Your Current Stage of Development

Learn what is important to you.

Set limits, priorities, and boundaries and stick to them.

Recognize that discomfort and pain are part of life.

Learn mindfulness so you can learn the difference between being mindful versus being numb. It will provide a way for you to be aware of your feelings so you can process them instead of diminishing and denying them.

In Relationships (For Your Partner's Understanding)

Just because your partner did not say "no" does not mean they mean "yes."

Nines are most likely to say the things they think you want to hear, whether they agree or not.

They make decisions that will make others happy before themselves.

Pay close attention to what your partner normally enjoys and offer to do the activities you know they will appreciate.

Show appreciation when you know they are trying to appease and please you.

Chapter 5:

Enneagram Type Partnerships

How the Types Behave When Paired Together

This section will provide an overview of the relationship dynamics between each of the enneatype pairings. Every single potential match will be covered, and each section will cover how the two will naturally be together based on their respective types, the positive characteristics of each other and the relationship that can come out in their pairing, and conversely the negative if unhealthy levels of development are expressed. You will find that often the same innate traits that can yield positive results if expressed by a healthy individual in a healthy manner, can turn negative if expressed by an unhealthy individual in an unhealthy manner. Through awareness, this information can show you where you fall in the spectrum. Though everything may not apply to you, this will show you the ideal version of your relationship that you can strive for, and will aid you in avoiding potential pitfalls that can lead to the demise of the relationship.

*Note: Every pairing is covered, but it is not repeated. To avoid repeat information, higher number enneatypes will have to refer to the lower number enneatype sections to find their pairing.

1 & 1

Double Type Ones

Overview

Both people will usually bring the same general qualities to the relationship since they share a common type. This can either be a major attraction or a potential disaster. They each have high standards they expect the other to keep. Because of these high expectations, they could not handle being in a relationship with someone whose character was not stellar.

Both partners will expect important responsibilities to come first. Pleasurable activities and relationship growth will always rank low and many times become neglected. Often, a common interest will bring two Type Ones together. Type One couples benefit from sharing a common goal.

Potential Trouble

Type Ones can easily become judgmental and intolerant of mistakes or immaturity in their partner. They are highly aware of the short-comings of both their partner and the relationship.

Instead of turning against each other, two Ones may double-team against the world. Double Ones can bring the other down to an unhealthy level of development. They may find themselves isolated from others who do not live up to their expectations.

1 & 2

Type One with Type Two

Overview

Type One and Type Two personalities can complement each other. Both types are interested in helping others. However, this can also become a stress point because they may focus too much attention on other people, rather than their own relationship. They are very mature and independent. They fulfill their emotional needs from outside connections. They keep their relationship strong by sticking to high ideals and strong ethical standards. Many times, they use the power of two to increase their ability to help others.

This type of relationship provides elements that both types are searching for. The Type Two personality helps the Type One personality to relax. They provide nurturing and compassion that the Type One desires but refuses to indulge in themselves. The Type One provides structure to the relationship, making the Type Two feel secure. The Type Two personality is generally more empathetic toward while the Type One personality has the ideas and discernment to know what the other person needs.

Potential Trouble

Type Ones tend to be unaware of their needs while Type Twos become too involved serving others to tend to their needs. Therefore, both types find it hard to express their needs in the relationship. Neither type will admit they are not satisfied because both types feel striving for their own needs is selfish and forbidden. The Type One personality may resent the Type Two personality for giving too much time and attention to others instead of investing in the relationship.

The Type Two personality may feel the Type One personality is too impersonal in his/her dealings with others. Type Twos feel that while Type Ones are on a mission to improve humanity, Type Ones have little to no compassion for individuals. Both types can become critical of each other.

1 & 3

Type One with Type Three

Overview

Both types are serious minded, idealistic, and competent. This type of relationship has the capacity to be task-oriented and driven by hard work. They both have high expectations for themselves and the relationship. They are more open to discussing issues since neither type likes having unresolved issues in their life.

Type Ones help Threes to be more realistic and grounded. Type Threes help Ones stretch their comfort zones and encourage Type Ones not to be so perfectionistic. Both types are persistent and industrious. They are concerned with excellence and efficiency and have high goals to make a real difference in the world.

Potential Trouble

The major areas of concern for this type of relationship are lack of emotional attachment, time commitments, or even a sense of competition. Ones tend to accuse Threes of being insincere in their achievements. Ones tend to feel Type Threes lack principle, and are more concerned with the bottom line of achieving a goal or purpose.

Type Threes generally feel Ones are inflexible and too judgmental in their attitudes. Type Threes may value the Ones' organizational ability to get things done. However, Threes often feel Type Ones are too focused on the details rather than the results. Both may gradually lose respect for the other person. Type Ones lose respect for Type Threes' integrity, while Type Threes lose respect for Ones' effectiveness.

If dating, a break in the relationship is possible, however, if married, it is more likely that a married Type One and Type Three will stay in a failing marriage for continued personal status.

1 & 4

Type One with Type Four

Overview

These two types both have a mutual interest in improving the world around them. Both are idealists. Both types can see how things could be if someone like them brought about a change to improve things.

Ones bring a desire for truth, reason, and objectivity to the relationship. They also offer good work habits, self-discipline, and regularity to the relationship. Ones are conscientious and will redirect themselves and their needs to focus on the greater good.

Ones can become a sounding board for Type Fours. They can offer advice and clarity when the Four's judgment is clouded by their feelings or self-doubt.
Fours bring to the relationship creativity, spontaneity, inspiration, sensuality, intense feelings, and the ability to tap into universal forces such as dreams or the unconscious. Their emotionality and expressiveness can provide a counterbalance to Type One's formality and sense of order and reason.

Ones help Type Fours bring their dreams to completion by supporting the Four's creativity with structure. Ones bring self-restraint to the relationship. This is a great model for Fours because they tend to be more unregulated with their dreams and ideals.

Both types have a desire for refinement and cultivation of the arts. If both partners can appreciate the strengths of each other, they can make a productive team, balancing out each other's limitations.

Potential Trouble

Sometimes the relationship between Type Ones and Type Fours is like mixing oil and water—they separate because they perceive ideas from different points of view. Ones are always sensible and objective, while Fours would rather see things from a personal side rather than with objectiveness.

Their idealism may not align. Ones are idealistic about external causes while Fours' ideals are focused on themselves and their relationships.
Both can be condescending toward others who do not see things the same way they do. Eventually, they can turn their condescending attitude toward each other.

While both types are aware of their impulses, sensuality, and longings, they tackle the issues in opposite ways. Ones try to repress their impulses while Fours use their impulses to obtain their goals. Therefore, one of the biggest areas of conflict is self-discipline versus self-indulgence.

Ones begin to see Fours as self-absorbed and hopelessly emotional. Fours see Type Ones as rigid and judgmental. While things like lack of trust, intimacy, or communication are common reasons why relationships end, a One and Four relationship may end by being disgruntled with each other for being the way they are.

1 & 5

Type One with Type Five

Overview

Ones and Fives are alike in many ways. Both types repress their emotions and see themselves as fact-oriented. They both avoid letting their emotions cloud their judgment.

Ones and Fives typically enjoy each other's company because they admire each other's intelligence and expertise. They love to laugh together at life's irrationalities. Both types highly respect personal boundaries. Neither one would make the first move unless they knew it would be appreciated by the other. Therefore, these types tend to bring formality and courtesy to each other.

Ones bring logic and order while Fives bring curiosity. When romance develops, it develops slowly but intensely.

Potential Trouble

Although both types are intellectual and alike in many ways, they can also be opposites in areas which are important to them, leading to conflict and potential break of the relationship. Ones are concerned with objectiveness and the ultimate truth. However, Fives do not believe in objective truth. Rather, they believe there are multiple interpretations of the truth. At unhealthy levels of development, Ones can become fundamentalists while Fives can become anarchists, denying the truth altogether.

Both types have a difficult time changing their basic philosophies and lose respect for anyone who challenges their ideas. However, both types respect each other's boundaries to a fault. This can cause the relationship to become impersonal and distant. Ones may feel Type Fives are too impractical while Fives may feel type Ones are rigid, taking their opinions too seriously. Both types can become too self-contained to contribute any energy toward the relationship.

1 & 6

Type One with Type Six

Overview

Type Ones and Sixes are alike in several ways to the point they are often misidentified with each other. Both types have a strong sense of duty. They are conscientious and hard workers. Both types have a desire to serve people and improve the world.

Ones bring reason and clarity to the relationship. They are confident in their actions and opinions and tend to take on the leadership role in the relationship. Sixes offer emotional availability and bring warmth to the relationship. Their playfulness and generosity may cause Type Ones to think twice about their beliefs. Sixes have more empathy to connect with people than Type Ones do. Sixes take responsibility and share the burdens and chores. They are faithful and loyal to each other.

When their fundamental beliefs are aligned, these qualities can create a dynamic and highly stable team. Both types want to build a solid foundation together. Since they feel they can count on each other, it gives both people room to relax.

Potential Trouble

When there is stress in their life, Ones become all work and no play and criticize anyone who doesn't take their work as seriously as they do. Too much arguing will wear down Type Sixes much more than it does Type Ones. When Sixes are stressed, they react emotionally and attempt to turn to their partner for stability. Instead, Type Ones can add to the Six's anxiety by being too critical. Sixes may create a self-fulfilling prophecy of doom to the relationship. Many times, Sixes will become defensive and evasive. They will find external activities to avoid spending time with their critical partner. They find it too difficult to talk about their anxieties in the relationship.

As Type Ones become more resentful of the Type Six personality, resolute Sixes will only do the minimum to contribute to the relationship. The stubbornness of Type Sixes drives Ones into fits of frustration. Resentment, anger, and name calling can arise between these two personalities as the relationship deteriorates.

1 & 7

Type One with Type Seven

Overview

These two types are complementary opposites, which can go one of two ways in the relationship. They can either bring something needed for growth to the other person or push the other person away by using their weakness against them. Sevens offer Ones a sense of excitement, while Ones bring a sense of purpose and direction. Ones take pleasure in maintaining high standards. Sevens bring spontaneity and curiosity. Sevens take pleasure in fun and adventure. They don't get hung up on all the details of doing things perfectly. Sevens appreciate Type One's reliability and attention to detail, but they help Ones stay lighthearted and prevent the relationship from becoming too serious.

One commonality between the types is they are idealistic in their plans. However, Sevens prefer having multiple options to get the job done while Type Ones believe there's only one right way to accomplish their ideas. Ones believe they are keeping Sevens focused and resistant to distraction by minimizing their options. Sevens value freedom and spontaneity, while Ones make sure the job gets done efficiently. Their differences help them support each other's goals and productivity. This can be a highly supportive relationship when their goals in life are aligned.

Potential Trouble

Ones can become too inflexible and insist things are only done their way. They see Type Sevens as childish. Ones feel that Sevens are scattered and fool around too much. They feel Type Sevens over extend resources and promise too much to too many people. They believe Sevens can act this way on purpose to passive aggressively get back at the Type One for some reason. Sevens see Type Ones as perfectionistic and believe they need to loosen up.

Conflicts are typically centered around organizational and financial matters. Ones feel that Sevens are reckless and wasteful. Sevens see Ones as too tight-fisted with no real vision.

Ones may lose respect for Type Sevens and find them embarrassing to be around, leading them to ultimately withdraw emotional connection from their partner. Sevens will pursue other options when they feel trapped by the One's constant criticism and dissatisfaction. Disdain and contempt make reconciliation difficult between these types.

1 & 8

Type One with Type Eight

Overview

Both types fight for truth and justice. They see themselves as crusaders, making the world a better place. They feel it is up to them to fix injustices, but unfortunately, they often have different methods for fixing the problems they perceive.

They are action-oriented and can bring about significant changes when working together for social causes. They are both perseverant and bring purpose and practicality to their missions. Both types are willing to suffer for the greater good, if necessary.

Type Eights bring a practical and immediate approach to the One's ideals.
This powerful combination can achieve results with purpose and clear personal mission. Eights provide passion that counterbalances the One's self-restraint. Eights understand the determination of Ones and understand Ones are not easily swayed from their ideals.

Eights are attracted to the challenge of getting close to Ones. They can be opposite but can learn from each other if they are open-minded to the other's methods and values.

Potential Trouble

The differences between these types are like fire (Eights) and ice (Ones), yet both types want to be in charge.

Ones may see Type Eights as rogue outlaws and may admire their bravado but abhor the chaos and destruction Ones feel it will create.

Eights often see Ones as hypocrites who preach one thing but don't keep their private behaviors in check. They see Ones as self-righteous, rigid and unrealistic about the way the world works. This may cause Eights to act out to provoke the One's judgmental nature.

Both types deny hurt and fear. Instead, they react with anger.

This type of relationship can often end with violent arguments and personal attacks on each other. This can be a difficult relationship to repair.

1 & 9

Type One with Type Nine

Overview

These types understand each other on a personal level because they see many of their own traits in each other. They both bring idealism and desire for change. Both can be hard working and willing to put their own needs aside for the welfare of others.

Nines are gentle, providing nurture and support. They prefer harmony rather than taking pleasure in being right, like a One. Nines help mitigate the critical nature and seriousness of Ones, while Ones provide clarity and direction for Nines. Ones excel in articulating their ideas.

This can be a very philanthropic couple, balancing idealism with humanity.

Nines soothe Ones, while Ones remind Nines to strive for excellence.

Their love for nature, animals, and family brings them closer together.

Potential Trouble

The main conflict between these types is how they handle conflict and stress. Ones are more open about their frustration with others when things don't go their way, but they obsess over who is at fault and what needs to change for improvement. Nines, on the other hand, are withdrawn and shut down under stress. Nines may tune out Ones and deny there's a problem. Ones will blame Nines for not taking enough responsibility to fix problems.

The more Ones push Nines to respond in a certain way, the more Nines become unable to succumb to the One's ways. Nines will retreat to passive aggressive behavior. Ones perceive the Nine's behavior as resistance and negligence.
Ones lose respect for Nines and Nines become uncomfortable expressing themselves with Ones. Ones will become more self-righteous while Nines become unresponsive.

If they're not careful, their anger will eventually get the better of them and end the relationship.

2 & 2

Double Type Twos

Overview

Healthy Two couples bring a high level of affection, sensitivity, and warmth to the relationship. Their genuine concern for the relationship and their partner makes them able to put a lot of energy into making sure all problems are resolved. Double Two relationships have a high level of communication. They frequently check on their partner to make sure all is well.

Since neither partner in a double Two relationship is accustomed to being nurtured by others, they need to learn to allow themselves to be loved and helped by the other person. If each of the Twos can allow the support of the other, the relationship can become a source of deep love and abundance.

Healthy Twos are generous and respectful of boundaries. They understand the need for independence and individual growth while offering any resources they can to help their partner succeed. They express enormous affection but can also let go, creating balance between themselves as a couple versus as individuals.

Double Twos feel secure and loyal. They know their partner will be there to help them when they need it most.

This can be a loving and warm-hearted couple that provides security for their family and helps make the world a more loving place. This type of couple may also be open to adopting children and providing their love to those who need it most.

Potential Trouble

Intimate relationships could pose a problem for double Twos. Their need for validation from others sets them up for secret jealousy and competition for the center of attention. They may become jealous if someone chooses their partner for advice or social events.

Twos may try to charm those around them to get a reaction, which can get in the way of an exclusive intimate relationship. Some Twos may begin to lose interest in themselves and their looks. Others may turn to other people or food to cater to their desire for intimacy. This can cause both parties to lose physical interest in the relationship and in each other.

Unhealthy Twos are likely to develop boundary problems. They will either get overly enmeshed with each other, or one may become repulsed by their partner's hovering. Isolation, loneliness, depression, and dealing with blame can become the result of a relationship between unhealthy double Twos.

2 & 3

Type Two with Type Three

Overview

Most of the time, both types are driven by their emotional needs. However, Type Threes are not as driven by feeling as Type Twos. Both yearn for attention and the desire to be loved, however, Twos are not always as concerned for their own needs for attention and love.

Both types can become preoccupied with activities that put them in the spotlight among other people. These types are sociable, charming, and high-spirited. They know how to get the attention of others and leave a favorable impression on others around them. Each type brings energy, ambition, and the ability to communicate to the relationship. They know how to make the other feel special like they are the center of attention.

Type Twos are more personal in their interactions with others. They are thoughtful and follow through with kindness and compassion. Threes provide practicality, charm, flexibility, and goal-oriented structure for ways the couple can improve.

This type of pairing can make for a special, and very complimentary relationship. Type Twos like feeling proud of their loved ones, while Type Threes strive to make their partner proud. Twos enjoy letting others be in the spotlight, while Threes enjoy being in the spotlight. Type Twos are content to be the power behind the throne, while Threes prefer to be on the throne. If healthy Threes appreciate the extravagant attention from the Type Two, this can be a near perfect pairing.

Potential Trouble

While some aspects of this pairing may be near perfect, every relationship has potential for problems. This couple type has the potential to become self-conscious and even more so of their partner.

The Two personality may become jealous and possessive of Threes. They can develop a feeling of "I made you – you owe me" toward the Type Three. Type Twos may feel unappreciated and used by Type Threes. Type Twos may appear as if they enjoy taking a back seat to the Three's success, but depending on their level of development, they can secretly want to be recognized and feel important, but refuse to admit it verbally. This is challenging because Threes find it difficult to thank others and share the glory. Additionally, Threes feel that Twos attempt to take too much credit for their contributions.

Both types tend to feel shame and vulnerability. They exploit and attempt to take advantage of their partner's weaknesses. Type Twos may undermine the Three's confidence because the Two wants to feel needed by the Three. Threes distance themselves from their partner if they feel humiliation or criticism. This creates additional anxiety for the Two and leads to manipulation.

Both types have a hard time admitting or realizing what they truly want and need on a deeper level. In a relationship, they may assume they want the same things and are moving in that direction, when they may in fact be drifting apart. Type Twos feel neglected when Threes put other activities, such as their career, before their home and family. Twos feel Type Threes should be more focused on internal values, like love, instead of external values, like success and fame. Home and family are very important to Twos, and they cannot understand how anyone could put other duties before their home, family, and what they believe "truly matters."

Threes can feel smothered and manipulated by Twos. They feel stifled by the Twos' constant need to be together and feel guilty for trying to provide a successful life for their family. This couple needs to define what success in a relationship means to them to work things out and be successful.

2 & 4

Type Two with Type Four

Overview

Intimacy and openness are the first hurdles this couple will need to overcome. Once they are willing to share their feelings openly, this can be a passionate relationship. Healthy Twos and Fours seek warmth and connection and are willing to provide it to each other. This type of relationship can provide a haven for each party to share their intimate desires without criticism. They can be exactly what the other type needs.

Twos provide the energy to be sociable, which gives their Four partner more confidence when interacting with others. Twos are warm, considerate, encouraging, generous, and thoughtful. They are also willing to help and contribute however they can. They are practical and action-oriented.

Fours bring creativity, emotional honesty, and a sense of humor to the relationship. They are willing to laugh at life's faults. They openly admit their own faults to themselves and their partner. Fours care about the impact things have on themselves and others. They have a way of bringing sensitivity to emotions and sensuality to the relationship. Fours also bring a sense of unpredictability and mystery.

Fours provide an environment that allows Twos to feel more nurtured and relaxed. Fours encourage Twos to discover their deeper needs and discover their true self, something Twos typically avoid on their own. Twos appreciate the nuances and subtleness of Fours, and Fours will thrive when they feel they are being appreciated.

Together, these two types can appreciate their quirks, and lighten the mood with humor, not taking themselves too seriously. Each person allows the other to mature emotionally. Both types help each other become more internally focused and less concerned with external criticism.

Potential Trouble

While this seems like a potentially perfect pairing on the surface, if these two are not intentional about sharing their feelings, there can be many unspoken demands and emotions, which can undermine the success of the relationship. While their common emotional issues may allow them to be more understanding of each other, it also sets up the potential for conflict. Both types desire intimacy and closeness. They will cling to anyone who will accept their attention. Over time, they may become competitive for their friends' and family's affections.

Type Twos often find Fours to be temperamental and moody. They feel Fours are too self-absorbed to care about the feelings and needs of others. Fours believe Twos are not as genuine as they want people to believe. They have a perception that Twos bribe people for attention with their helpfulness. Fours are often jealous of the Twos' social skills and ability to easily get the attention the Fours really want. Fours will begin to feel overshadowed by the popularity of their partner. It can exacerbate the Fours' feelings of abandonment when their partner becomes too involved with other people.

Both partners may develop feelings of shame and worthlessness, which will undermine the relationship. Both partners may feel their partner is too needy emotionally and not worth the effort to continue in the relationship.

2 & 5

Type Two with Type Five

Overview

These types are striking opposites. The Type Two is a "feeling" type and a people person. The Type Five is a "thinking" type and more of a loner. Each person has different perspectives on what is important in both life and a relationship. Their striking differences present a unique challenge to each other.

Twos will be the ones to make the first move in initiating contact. They are enthralled with the challenge of trying to charm the Five. Healthy Twos offer warmth, ease, and physical comfort. They want to improve the Five's lifestyle, even though Fives have no problem with it. While they may not show it, Fives enjoy the attention and the feeling that someone cares. Twos take pride in warming up the Five, and Fives secretly enjoy the nurture and attention they may have previously given up on finding.

Fives are very loyal. They value any relationship that seems to be working because they typically find relationships too difficult to enjoy. Fives bring stability and calmness to the relationship. They have good judgment and the ability to be objective in a crisis. They do not dwell on the outcome of a situation; instead, they are good advisors and make wise decisions. Fives can also be good listeners and provide their undivided attention. They are calmer and more emotionally stable than Twos.

Potential Trouble

Respect for each other's boundaries is a common problem for this type of relationship. Type Twos get frustrated when Fives do not respond to them quickly. Fives are reserved and too involved in their own mental world and may not respond at all. The Type Two personality will perceive this as rejection which will trigger fears of being unwanted and unloved. Twos may try even harder to break the Five's shell.

This type of intrusion by the Two is detrimental to the Five. Fives will detach emotionally and become withdrawn when they feel their sanctuary of inner peace is being threatened. The more distant the Five becomes, the more the Two becomes obsessed with pursuing the Five. This chase for space and capture is a prescription for disaster and loneliness.

Twos in the lower levels of development feel they are worthless when they aren't entangled in every aspect of the other person's life. Fives will perceive Twos as being irrational and out of control. Fives will become cynical about the practicality and value of being in a relationship, and may conclude that relationships just won't work for them.

2 & 6

Type Two with Type Six

Overview

Twos and Sixes are both dutiful toward others. They take their responsibilities very seriously. Both put the needs of others ahead of their own needs They are both family types. Both enjoy ensuring the welfare of their family, children, and closest friends. They are highly involved with their community and understand the strength that comes from having reliable social connections.

The loyalty of Twos makes them a strong contender for the position of a spouse for Sixes and a good parent for their children. Sixes value the self-sacrifice and generosity of Twos. Twos focus on fostering positive emotions and intimacy. Sixes attempt to construct a secure foundation for the couple. The Type Two has admiration for the perseverance and hard work of the Type Six.

The Two will rely on the Six's watchfulness to recognize difficulties before they become potential problems. A relationship between Twos and Sixes typically becomes based on mutual respect for each other's steadiness. They may consider each other "the safe choice."

Potential Trouble

Lower functioning Sixes lack the confidence to be decisive when solving problems. They become anxious when they feel pressured by too many forces. When Twos attempt to help Sixes work through their anxiety, it is perceived as just being additional orders, and adds to the pressure they feel. Sixes perceive Twos as undermining them and their ability to conquer their problems.

Lower functioning Twos believe there can't be too much intimacy. They strive to feel closer to their partner. Sixes send mixed messages, pushing the Two away, before pulling them back in. This activates the

Two's feelings of rejection, so they try to "help" even more. Sixes perceive the Two's "help" as being control, and seek distance instead of closeness. The back and forth behavior of Sixes may destroy the mutual respect the Two once had for them.

2 & 7

Type Two with Type Seven

Overview

Twos and Sevens can be outgoing, funny, friendly, and high-energy. They make for enjoyable company. These types want everyone to have fun and be happy. Both types appreciate the goodness in life and look for the positive in all situations. They are spontaneous and engaging. These qualities can make for a very fun, light hearted relationship.

Twos help Sevens feel relaxed. Sevens feel Twos adequately fulfill their emotional and physical needs.

Twos expect every day to be an adventure with Sevens, and for good reason. The Seven's high energy translates to a quick mind that can devise plans quicker than they can be acted on. Sevens seem to radiate mental electricity and excitement, which Twos find intoxicating. They admire the gusto of Sevens to forge ahead in life.

Both types are idealistic and Sevens enjoy sharing abundance with others, however, Twos are more likely to translate this kind of idealistic impulse into altruistic action. They are concerned with the welfare of others, but the Seven will remind the Two that they cannot fully help others unless they help themselves first. Together, they form a generous and thoughtful couple and can have a remarkably positive effect on those around them.

Potential Trouble

Twos feel they never have enough intimacy. They find ways to get closer to the Seven, which can lead them to become more clingy. As a result, Sevens begin to feel trapped and lose interest in the relationship. Twos will want a deeper relationship, but begin to perceive Sevens as untrustworthy and incapable of commitment. Sevens perceive Twos as manipulative and possessive. Sevens can become unsettled and upset by the idea of settling down. They see it as a limitation. Sevens are capable of long term commitment but do not actively seek it.

Sevens need to be the center of attention to stay excited and energized. If they do not feel they are getting this attention in their relationship, they can go outside of it to satisfy that need, causing Twos to feel used. Twos can react by withholding affection, overeating, or developing health problems. The unhealthy behaviors of these types lead to a deadlock with both parties hurt emotionally.

2 & 8

Type Two with Type Eight

Overview

Twos and Eights can be sentimental and compassionate, with a tender side that is often hidden. Both can play the roles of protector, provider, nurturer, and caretaker. Both types are likely to deny their own desires and needs. They tend to overwork themselves, and they each want to be the strength of the relationship. Twos may become the emotional leader, while Eights make all the practical decisions.

Each type brings vitality, passion, interpersonal and social capabilities, nobility, and generosity. However, Twos can be more concerned with the welfare of others, while Eights can be more concerned with physical well-being and having a noticeable effect on their world.

They may take on roles that the opposite wants and needs: Eights are practical and results driven, while Twos are more social and more philanthropic. They are both strong minded and like assuming responsibility, if they select the responsibilities themselves. Eights soak up the adoration and affection of Twos. Two appreciate the Eight's power and efforts. Both types see each other's noble characteristics and may be each other's loyal supporters and admirers. Their roles are also clearly defined, so they do not get in each other's way.

Twos and Eights are exceptional at keeping each other and their relationship well balanced. These features make them powerful allies who complement each other's strengths, especially the good effects they have on others.

Potential Trouble

Twos and Eights have different relationship styles. Twos are empathic and indirect. While Eights are independent and direct. Even Eights with an average level of development are proud of their unsentimental way of dealing with situations and people. Twos can become too attached to people and over-solicitous about their needs.

Eights are concerned with their own self-interests, while Twos are concerned with other people's interests. Eights see people as weak if they cannot take care of themselves. This can cause significant conflict over the importance of other people (including family) in the relationship.

Both types seem to have opposing views and move in opposite directions, especially concerning the treatment of others. Eights are callous and confrontational, while Twos are self-sacrificial and possessive. Twos will feel as if they must apologize for their partner's behavior.

Their conflicts are centered around who's methods are the best. Lost respect will spell the end of the relationship between these types.

2 & 9

Type Two with Type Nine

Overview

Twos and Nines are very similar in their ideals. Both types are concerned with other people, and go out of their way to be considerate of others. They both want to create peace and help those around them. Both types can find positives from experiences and see the positives in others. They are both easy going, friendly, hospitable, undemanding, and welcoming. Their home, pets, and environment are important to them.

Twos are more extroverted than Nines. Twos like to get down to details with people. Nines are more steady and quiet. They are more likely to get directly to the point than Twos.

Nines have a way of being calming and providing unquestioned acceptance. Both types are attracted by each other's soothing support. Their best communication is through physical closeness. They can develop nearly psychic communication with each other. They are a very mellow couple. Their hospitality is healing to themselves and to others.

Potential Trouble

Both types are used to giving up their power to others. However, for a successful relationship, it's essential to have a leader. Negotiating power can be stressful for both types. Neither one wants to be the "bad guy." The Type Two partner may step into the "boss" role but it usually doesn't fit well with them, and they may become too controlling.

Neither type is comfortable talking about how they feel. Nines struggle with speaking up for themselves, but when they do, Twos will feel threatened and offended. Twos do not accept criticism well. Since Nines don't typically speak up and feel like their feelings are heard, they may go overboard with resentments that continue to build up. Nines will withdraw and become passive-aggressive to deal with their frustration.

The couple seems like they have everything together on the outside, while deep down they have drifted apart. Neither wants to accept responsibility or talk about the failure of the relationship.

3 & 3

Double Type Threes

Overview

Double Threes are concerned with achievement and excellence. They are hard workers and always want to improve their status in life and share their rewards with others. Threes are charmers and charm their way into people's lives. Some Threes may be less sociable and more concerned with financial security.

Two Threes can form a very effective team, capable of success no matter what they pursue. They can coordinate tasks to increase their effectiveness as a team. Double Threes motivate each other to aim higher in their goals and achievements. They want their partner to be proud of them. All they expect in return is respect and acknowledgment of their personal achievements.

Threes prefer to avoid drama, and try to give their partner space to develop their own interests. Threes are known for the longevity of their relationships and their closeness and devotion to others.

Potential Trouble

Healthy Threes are highly supportive of each other, however problems arise in lower levels of development. Threes are known to become competitive and try to one-up their partner. Their jealousy and competition can undermine the support and pride they had for their partner. It is common for Threes to compare their income and their success at work. They may use their personal and professional successes to make their partner feel inferior.

Threes who may not have had serious relationships in the past may blame their partner for taking them away from their work. When they both focus their attention on work, they may neglect their pets, children, family, and friends. Threes have been so accustomed to burying themselves in work that they neglect their emotional and personal needs. They may not know what they truly want in life (besides success).

Eventually, their competition to be the best in the relationship leads to isolation and depression, causing the relationship to drift apart.

3 & 4

Type Three with Type Four

Overview

This can be a complementary pairing. Each type brings important qualities the other lacks. Fours can teach Threes how to communicate on a deeper level and learn to process their feelings. They also bring sensitivity, a sense of beauty, and an appreciation for fulfilling but "non-practical" aspects of life. Fours may help Threes increase their self-awareness and find their heart's desire. Fours also have a sense of style and refinement. They can bring rich communication to the relationship.

Threes have many of the qualities Fours desire for themselves. Threes are well-suited to share their achievements and help Fours develop new skills. Threes have tact when it comes to communicating with Fours, which can be crucial to building trust. Threes can bring a sense of ambition and practicality to the relationship. They can coach Fours through their slumps and times where they experience a lack of energy. In general, they are good at coaching Fours on both practical and professional matters.

Both Threes and Fours are in the feeling center of the Enneagram which can create an intense and passionate pairing. They may experience a connection that goes beyond words and reason.

Potential Trouble

Both types have issues with self-esteem. They both need validation and attention from others. They each question their identity and hide their feelings of worthlessness and shame. They often try to compare themselves and may initiate competitiveness between each other. The extent of their competitiveness will depend on how much they vie for personal approval, recognition, and attention.

Threes and Fours both need to feel appreciated. However, Threes may seek it more openly than Fours. Fours, unable to provide the desired feeling of appreciation that their Three partner needs, may begin to feel lacking and defective. Fours will typically devote more attention to the relationship than Threes. Fours desire more emotional intimacy than Threes are willing to provide. Both types are prone to hostility when their emotional needs are not met.

Another crucial problem is both types idealize their partner for who they want them to be rather than who they really are. Fours need a rescuer and someone who embodies the qualities they lack personally. Threes see Fours as a trophy to enhance their image and status to others.

If there is no respect and admiration within the relationship, they will begin to undermine the other and become dismissive. Toward the end of the relationship, these types become sarcastic and snippy to each other. They begin complaining about their partner's faults to their friends. After the relationship ends, they may try to sabotage the other out of revenge.

3 & 5

Type Three with Type Five

Overview

This is a common, but unexpected, pairing. Fives give Threes intellectual depth. They spark creativity within Threes. Threes help Fives cultivate the professional skills they need, such as confidence and how to communicate more effectively.

Threes have unique social skills. They use charm, practicality, and energy to sell their ideas to others. They can anticipate the skills needed to achieve success, both personally and professionally. Both types are preoccupied with being competent and effective, therefore, they tend to put their work ahead of their feelings.

Together, the couple can be competent, successful, and well respected. They can be a trophy for their partner depending on the development of their attractive strengths. They both see their partner as someone who can enhance their social status. They understand the balance between personal space and closeness, so they don't crowd each other.

Potential Trouble

The emphasis on work and competency shared by this couple may ultimately lead to jealousy and competitiveness, since they both assess their self-worth based on their success with work and how others perceive them professionally. Threes want to show off their professional achievements, while Fives want to show off their intellectual competency. It is common for these types to compare and even criticize each other's work.

Threes' insistence upon succeeding professionally can lead them to attempt to do so "by any means necessary," which can cause the Five to lose respect for their Three partner and question their ethics and honesty.

These types are reluctant to discuss their feelings and uncertainties about their relationship until it's too late. When they do communicate, their communication is ineffectual. Fives can be too argumentative and blunt. Threes will retaliate with sarcasm and criticism. Both types may be impatient and arrogant with each other.

Turning the relationship around will depend on their shared values and how valuable they see their partner to their status and needs. Otherwise, it is near impossible to restore the relationship once their connection is broken because both types are cynical and tend to be suspicious of others in general.

3 & 6

Type Three with Type Six

Overview

This pairing is not as common as it should be. Threes and Sixes work well together as a team. Common goals typically bring Threes and Sixes together. They both value tangible achievements.

Threes bring hard work, energy, optimism, and a desire to communicate. They are confident in their potential to succeed, both individually and as a couple. Sixes are more grounded. They respect diligence, perseverance, and loyalty. Sixes provide support, warmth, and practicality. Sixes also have compassion for others. Threes may learn to let their guard down and become more compassionate after being around a Six.

Both types foster mutual respect and admiration for the other's special talents and interests. Threes encourage Sixes in their confidence. Sixes offer support without smothering Threes. Sixes may encourage Threes to become a part of something bigger and think about more than just themselves.

Their heart-centered values and principles keep them grounded, establishing a relationship that has high potential for success.

Potential Trouble

Despite possessing the qualities each other needs, they can also bring out the worst qualities if they are in unhealthy levels of development. They tend to have similar negative qualities in common since Type Three is a stress point for Type Six.

They both look to others for reassurance. They both want to be accepted and recognized socially. Both can be a type of conformist. Threes conform to others' ideas for success, while Sixes conform to the will of those around them.

They both put their own feelings aside to achieve success. Their coping styles aggravate each other because they remind each other of their own weak spots. Threes try to prove they're better than the Six. Sixes can become nervous and explode like a loose cannon on Threes. Sixes tend to be too cautious, while Threes are too ambitious.

At their worst, both types become dishonest and shady about their actions and feelings. They may develop a relationship that has become more robotic when they ignore their feelings.

Threes will attempt to keep appearances socially and become embarrassed if their Six partner divulges problems between them to outsiders. They eventually lose enthusiasm and interest in each other.

3 & 7

Type Three with Type Seven

Overview

No other pairing has the capability of being as gregarious and vivacious as a Three and Seven couple. They both have high energy, and are self-assertive, optimistic, future-oriented, and outgoing. Their energy makes them attractive to other people. Threes and Sevens are also articulate and persuasive.

Threes bring communication skills, empathy, decorum, and appropriateness. They focus on goals, healthy limits, practicality, and possess the ability to stay grounded. Sevens bring fun, resilience, spontaneity, and adventure. They are not overly concerned with failure, like Threes. Sevens bring vast knowledge and experience, coupled with enthusiasm and good spirits.

These two put all their energy and heart in a variety of activities and projects, with hopes of sustaining a comfortable lifestyle for their family. Being active and going out on adventures together is a great way for these two to bond, and these shared experiences that they both value can help bring out their full potential.

Threes and Sevens may seem like a magical pairing to others. And should things begin to go sour, Threes and Sixes have confidence in their ability to renew their relationship.

Potential Trouble

Threes and Sevens possess similar qualities that can camouflage their problems. They avoid talking about their insecurities for as long as possible, which often ends up being too long. It usually takes a crisis for their problems to surface. They can hurt each other unintentionally, and in an attempt to remain light-hearted, they hide their hurt until it consumes them and becomes too late to face it.

If unchecked, their energy and ambition can work against them and become explosive. Both want to keep up their perfect couple appearance, which eventually becomes exhausting. They value the image of the "power couple" and put tremendous pressure on themselves to emulate it.

Threes may become workaholics and focus on advancing their careers and building professional prestige, placing their partner on the back burner. Sometimes, it may seem like they forget about life outside of work. Threes can become jealous of the Seven's success. Feeling like they're falling behind at work and being neglected at home, resentment builds and the Seven can undermine the Three's pursuit of the perfect career and can grow to feel used by the Three.

Neither one wants to be in a monotonous relationship, nor have a failed relationship. So, they shift their focus to self-centered interests until the relationship eventually comes to an end.

3 & 8

Type Three with Type Eight

Overview

Threes and Eights can form powerful, passionate, highly effective, and stimulating partnerships. They are both persuasive and self-confident. They are both assertive and fight for what they want in life. Both types tend to stand out in their social cliques. When brought together, it is inevitable that they will notice each other.

Eights bring directness, physical vigor, fearlessness, decisiveness, and strength to the relationship. Eights enjoy watching Threes take charge and overcome challenges. Eights begin to relax when they understand Threes can take care of themselves. Threes gain confidence from the Eight.

Threes and Eights want to support each other and be proud of each other's accomplishments and potential. When their relationship is in a healthy state, they direct their competitiveness towards other people.

Eights are reliable, and Threes need that sense of security before they can let their guard down. The Eight's strength gives Threes the ability to be more sensitive. Threes are adaptable and know how to please.

Potential Trouble

With both types being workaholics, Threes and Eights battle for leadership and the determination of who supports who in the relationship. Under stress, they can become selfish. This causes them to prioritize their personal success over their relationship, which can lead them to compete with their partner, when they would usually support them.

Eights are more open about how controlling they are, but Threes use subtle forms of manipulation to control others, which can make Eights suspicious and lose respect and trust for Threes. After they lose trust, Eights become jealous and possessive. They order their partner to do things to prove loyalty. Eights will begin to demand loyalty until Threes feel like they can no longer pursue their own goals.

Eights may see the Three as untrustworthy and deceitful. Threes can see the Eight as vengeful and willful. Threes tend to feel used and belittled when they don't feel appreciation from their partner. Neither the Threes nor the Eight can express their feelings for fear of becoming vulnerable. Suspicion and isolation become their normal and is difficult to break, causing them to lose each other's trust completely. They are not afraid to cut their losses when things don't work out.

3 & 9

Type Three with Type Nine

Overview

This pair likes to avoid conflict and always seeks positivity. Nines genuinely look on the bright side with optimism. Threes focus on keeping a hopeful and positive attitude. Threes make sure no one sees them depressed or having a rough time. Threes and Nines are idealistic and sociable. They have a unique gift for caring for children and animals. Nines and Threes are hardworking, and want material success to enable them to take care of others. They desire an aesthetically pleasing home.

Nines bring encouragement, support, and pride in the Three's accomplishments. With the support of a Nine by their side, Threes can explore their potential and become the best version of themselves. Nines also assure Threes that they are loved for being themselves and not just for their achievements. Nines give Threes permission not to overwork themselves, and they help Threes relax and find enjoyment in simple things.

Nines bring steadiness, nonjudgment, and security. Threes bring ambition, energy, flexibility, goal management, and efficiency. They help Nines have more self-respect and learn to invest in themselves. They energize Nines and bring excitement and change to the relationship.

Potential Trouble

The Nine may be able to provide the materialistic and financial needs for the relationship, but may also feel like the Three is spoiled and too demanding. Threes may even feel that their success is stifled by the Nine.

On the surface, this kind of relationship may be "too much of a good thing." Both types are attracted to keeping life positive, causing them to suppress real issues. Threes and Nines are reluctant to bring up complaints. They don't want to disrupt their relationship with negative energy.

Nines can become emotionally absent. Sensing this distance, Threes can become depressed for fear of being rejected or abandoned, but are afraid to address the issue because of that very fear of being rejected by their partner. In times of conflict, Nines feel it is better to let things work themselves out without disturbing the peace.

It often takes an affair, crisis, or other major challenge to reveal the true state of the relationship. Threes and Nines are more likely to go through cycles of being "on again, off again." However, they won't have a successful relationship until they learn to become comfortable speaking up and communicating about their underlying problems.

4 & 4

Double Type Fours

Overview

Double Fours make good friends, and friendship is a great foundation for any romantic relationship. Typically, these two feel misunderstood by other personality types, but with each other, they feel relief due to a sense of understanding.

Fours more readily share intimate personal details, secrets, childhood experiences, dreams, and disappointments with each other. They are also open and sensitive to the needs of their partner and expect that same sensitivity to be reciprocated. Luckily, they can find it in other Fours.

They treat their relationship as a safe place where they can be open and honest. Their fear of being too different is relieved when they are with each other.

Potential Trouble

Emotional instability is the primary concern when dealing with Fours. They become self-absorbed in that they want their personal emotional issues to be the center of attention. Each person wants to feel special and be treated with "kid gloves" so to speak. However, they may resent their partner for wanting the same treatment. They both want someone who will rescue them from themselves.

Fours tend to withdraw from conflict and confrontation. Despite an awareness of issues in the relationship, Fours will tread softly around their partner, never really dealing with those issues. Fours may try to test their partner beyond what they can handle. They can become moody and passive-aggressive with the one person they were so in love with. Their arguments and micro aggressions will eventually damage the relationship past the point of no return.

4 & 5

Type Four with Type Five

Overview

Fours and Fives are private, and enjoy deep conversations and experiences. Fours have an artistic personality and an emotional temperament. Their habit of introspection enables them to be sensitive to their own feelings and their partner's feelings. Fives are inquiring and intellectual. They have a habit of asking questions and exploring vast interests. Both types appreciate each other's differences, and respect each other's commitment to follow their interests.

Fours and Fives are creative, and they love the stimulation received from sharing their discoveries with each other. They are sincerely interested in listening to their partner. Fours appreciate the effect new discoveries have on people. They understand the power of the Five's intellect to bring about enlightenment to the relationship and to others.

Fives introduce Fours to new worlds and new perspectives. Fours help Fives get in tune with their feelings. They inspire creativity in each other and encourage each other to be themselves. Both types enjoy humor and talking about bizarre and outlandish news. Their relationship may be described as quirky, unique, and full of character.

Potential Trouble

Fours feel that Fives are too impractical and take too long to take action, which can put stress on a home life if the pair is living together or married.

Intimacy versus personal space is the greatest conflict for Fours and Fives.
Fives tend to be more private and not ready for intimacy. Fours feel Fives are too intellectual to sympathize with their emotional. Fives feel drained by the Four's emotional needs. Fives feel Fours are too wrapped up in their feelings to be rational and can be unstable.

Fours get frustrated with the superficial attention (they feel) they get from Fives.

Unless Fives can learn to appreciate the Four's deep feelings, and Fours can learn to appreciate the Five's minimal emotions and boundaries, this type of relationship may not work out.

4 & 6

Type Four with Type Six

Overview

Sixes may misidentify as Fours due to the qualities they have in common. These similar qualities may be the cause of the very attraction bringing this couple together. Fours and Sixes gravitate towards each other because they both share an emotional nature and insecurity about themselves around people. Their commonalities create empathy and tolerance for each other. They may consider each other kindred souls. They also understand each other's distrust of others and fear of abandonment. Both let their intuition and feelings guide their decisions.

Fours and Sixes tend to support each other by allowing each other to vent their complaints and worries they would not feel comfortable discussing with others.

Fours bring sensuality, sensitivity, and the ability to express emotion to the relationship. Fours can teach Sixes how to express some of their emotions and how to talk about their personal issues.

Sixes bring hard work, practicality, perseverance, and loyalty. Due to their loyal nature, they can also express concern about the security of their relationship. Sixes are warm and playful and may be able to brighten the Four's spirit during down times. They give Fours space to develop their creativity, and give them support and time to work through emotional issues. Fours make Sixes feel needed, increasing the Six's confidence.

A relationship between Fours and Sixes at its best can help each partner seek higher levels of development.

Potential Trouble

Fours may welcome change by being interested in improving themselves as a person. They can also welcome adventure. However, Sixes are resistant to change, and therefore, Fours will perceive the Six as trying to hold them back. Fours desire more romance and free-spiritedness from Sixes. Sixes desire more dependability from Fours.

Feelings of abandonment typically lead to problems in this type of relationship. Fours and Sixes may become codependent, a hinderance to each person's personal growth. This unhealthy dependency is connected with lower self-esteem and the belief that they are nothing without the other.

In this type of relationship, problems and conflicts escalate quickly, leading to massive over reactions. Unhealthy Fours and Sixes may be pessimistic, critical, overwhelmed, and emotionally reactive. They will test each other's loyalty. Fours and Sixes can be self-doubting and mistrustful. They may prepare for the end by withdrawing their affection. However, many times, this creates a self-fulfilling prophecy.

4 & 7

Type Four with Type Seven

Overview

Fours and Sevens are intrigued by each other, representing a typical case of opposites attracting. Fours are introverted, quiet, self-doubting, pessimistic, and emotional. Sevens are extroverted, outgoing, self-confident, intellectual, and optimistic. Together, they highlight the contrast of their differences. They think differently. They react and find pleasure in different ways. Each finds the other's differences fascinating and intriguing.

Due to their opposite nature, they are likely to balance each other. Sevens are more "fun" and can help Fours overcome their shyness and their reluctance to try new experiences. Fours respect the Seven's feelings and keep Sevens focused on their true desires. Fours and Sevens invite ecstasy and joy, spontaneity, passion, and emotion.

Fours and Sevens can be irreverent, but funny and entertaining. They enjoy rich conversation and can pass hours communicating their thoughts, reactions, and even the mundane details of their life. They desire the finer things life has to offer – lavish food and wine, top of the line clothes and household furnishings, and travel. Many times, they overspend to accommodate their desired lifestyle. Fours and Sevens desire the latest and greatest. A dash of romance and adventure will keep their relationship fresh and lively. Their seemingly perfect lifestyle is an inspiration and joy to others.

Potential Trouble

There must be a strong force early in the relationship to keep these two types together. Otherwise, the relationship will fall apart quickly. Fours and Sevens are impulsive and easily frustrated when things don't go as planned. They have high expectations for the quality of attention they receive from their partner.

If they are not upfront about their complaints, neither type will give each other many chances to make up. Fours envy and admire the Seven's high energy and resilience. However, they are worn down quickly by the Seven's fast-paced lifestyle. Fours can perceive

Sevens as insensitive and superficial, and Sevens can perceive Fours as impractical. Sevens may try to imitate the Four's creativity and appreciation of beauty.

When the quality of the relationship worsens, Fours become hostile. Sevens become impatient and verbally abusive. Fours will want to talk things out. Sevens are quick to move on. By the end of the relationship, their cute quirks become irritating and insufferable to each other.

4 & 8

Type Four with Type Eight

Overview

This relationship will either be uniquely creative or innately volatile. Fours and Eights have strong emotional responses. They both act to get a reaction from their partner. They are both dominating. Eights are dominant in their interactions with people. Fours are dominant in their emotions.

Fours and Eights bring intensity, passion, subconscious feelings, and energy to all parts of the relationship. They are attracted to each other's hidden qualities, vulnerability, and even each other's storminess. Both types understand neither person are what they seem on the surface. Fours and Eights are highly intuitive. Fours are knowledgeable and self-aware of their feelings. Eights are intuitive about external occurrences.

Their passion can cause them to become reckless and impulsive, which can be exciting to them. However, with all exciting impulses, there's usually a trade-off. Fours depend on the practicality of Eights for provision and protection. Eights thrive on the challenge of getting inside the Four's emotional world.

Fours see charisma, strength, and solidity in Eights. Fours and Eights challenge themselves to live up to the other person's level of intensity. They make each other feel alive. Vitality, intensity, and passion are the emotional hallmarks of a relationship between these types.

Potential Trouble

Both take pride in being larger-than-life in different ways. Type Eight's strong willpower makes them seem larger-than-life, and Type Four's quest for self-expression and their strong connection to feelings make them seem larger-than-life.

Fours and Eights want to be free from control. They become quickly enraged if they feel pressured by someone else and don't feel free. They are both prone to depression, rage, and vengeance. Arguments and fighting become common in their relationship. They will withdraw affection and verbally condemn each other to "teach each other a lesson," many times in public to inflict shame and embarrassment. These types are known to drag outside family members into their squabbles and make them choose sides.

Their relationship can become a model of heated passion. Fours and Eights also enjoy the process of fighting just to make up. They find that the explosive conflict makes their relationship more exciting.

4 & 9

Type Four with Type Nine

Overview

Fours and Nines are private and withdrawn. They can also be sensitive to the needs and feelings of others. Both types are empathetic to those who are suffering. Fours and Nines are idealistic in search of their perfect soulmate. They desire a deep connection, but also want a sense of personal privacy.

Their lifestyle likely expresses their sensuality and desire to be comfortable in life. Fours and Nines are comfortable staying home and enjoying each other's company. They bring appreciation and passion for each other. They are both highly creative, and they support each other in their creative endeavors. They are willing to give each other the space they need to foster their talents.

Fours can help Nines express their feelings. Nines help the Four feel accepted and understood as a person. Fours are good at deciphering feelings. Nines will appreciate the Four's emotional storms and drama. The passion this couple has for each other is in the understanding of their emotions on a deeper level.

Potential Trouble

Nines abhor the Four's sense of entitlement. Fours despise the Nine's irresponsibility of not learning from their experiences.

Fours and Nines react differently to stress. Fours become demanding and emotionally volatile. Nines become disengaged. Nines will continue to shut down until communication is nonexistent. They don't want to hear about the Four's reactions or feelings. Fours see the relationship as boring. They start to feel contempt toward their partner and the relationship.

Fours and Nines seek partners who have strengths in the qualities they lack themselves. In unhealthy relationships between these types, their desires are not met, and they become stuck in the chaos of anger, irritation, and resentment with each other.

5 & 5

Double Type Fives

Overview

Double Fives seems like the perfect soulmates for each other. Fives stimulate each other's minds and are well informed. They are imaginative, independent, fact-oriented, and non-intrusive. Their idea of a perfect date night includes a good debate and a good movie.

Fives don't want to be controlled. Double Five relationships may be characterized by courtesy, respect for boundaries, and no expectations. They can provide each other with the space they need. They don't like people knowing things that are too personal about them, so they would never put someone on the spot by asking overly personal questions. They may be curious about others, but they have a hard time letting their guard down and trying to get themselves and others to open up emotionally.

Fives must learn to balance independence, intimacy, and sharing personal matters for their relationship to be successful. Once Fives find someone they feel comfortable with, they can become attached quickly. However, they may not be open about it right away, until they feel sure they won't be rejected.

Potential Trouble

Double Five relationships may become too intellectual. Fives may try to over analyze their partner, rather than try to identify with them.

They may also get in heated arguments over trivial matters. Each person feels their ideas and way of thinking is right, when in fact, the matter is so trivial and they may both be right, and it probably doesn't matter as much as they think.

They may try to designate strong boundaries and become secretive about their own intentions and personal life outside of the relationship. The emotional distance they put between themselves and their partner is typically the ultimate conflict in their relationship. They become too isolated from each other. They may even withdraw from the world around them as well.

5 & 6

Type Five with Type Six

Overview

Fives and Sixes are intellectual types with significant differences. They have respect for the intellectual insight, technical mastery, and expertise of their partner. It is not uncommon for them to begin their journey as colleagues before gradually developing into an intimate relationship over time.

Fives and Sixes respect attention to detail and accuracy, craftsmanship, and the skills to analyze situations without bias. Together, they can be effective in handling crises situations. They are watchful for potential problems and draw from their personal experience and expertise to solve them.

Fives offer detached objectivity, penetrating curiosity, and an unwillingness to settle for an answer without thoroughly testing it. Sixes bring high ideals and values that make them less objective but inject a sense of humanity. Sixes lack the self-confidence to make decisions. Therefore, they turn to experts for advice. Fives are skeptical of authority and rely on their own intuition.

The devotion and care of Sixes can help Fives let their guard down despite tending to isolate themselves. There must be unwavering trust for this type of pairing to work.

Potential Trouble

Fives and Sixes think and work in diametrically opposite ways, resulting in plenty of emotional and intellectual tension between them.

If the trust and communication between Fives and Sixes deteriorate, Fives begin to see Sixes as indecisive and too conventional. Sixes are then afraid to make a mistake within sight of their partner for fear of criticism and rejection.

Sixes may seem prejudicial, closed-minded, petty, and appeasers of authority rather than seekers of truth. Fives seem unwilling and unable to work with their partner as a team through life's issues. Sixes perceive the Five's ideas and methods as impractical and a waste of time.

They each contribute to each other's sense of hopelessness and powerlessness.
This pairing will take intentional hard work at building a solid relationship to be successful.

5 & 7

Type Five with Type Seven

Overview

Fives and Sevens bring a lot of intellectual energy and appreciation of ideas to a relationship. Each party brings qualities the other person is lacking.

Fives bring clarity, depth, insight, self-reliance, independence, and a whimsical sense of humor. They love knowledge and intellectual pursuits and have quick minds. Sevens bring quickness of spirit. They are ready for anything at the drop of a hat, and enjoy adventures with their friends. They are extravagant, generous, outgoing, gregarious, and the life of the party.

Fives tend to be more frugal with resources and money. Fives are private until you gain their trust. Fives keep Sevens grounded and encourage them to stick with their endeavors long enough to see if they will pay off. Sevens encourage Fives to come out of their shell and meet new people and try new experiences.

Fives and Sevens enjoy communication and exploring new places together. Their differences can balance each other out.

Potential Trouble

Fives minimize their expectations of life, especially during stress. They can detach and withdraw emotionally from their partner, causing them to become even more isolated and reclusive than already tends to be natural for their personality. The reactions of Sevens cause Fives to withdraw even more.

Sevens are accustomed to quick action and multiple backup plans and escape routes. As pressure increases, they keep trying to do more to distract them from their anxieties. Fives perceive Sevens as out of control. In extreme cases, the Five can fear the Seven.

In lower levels of development, Fives perceive Sevens as intrusive, superficial, and coarse. Sevens continue to try harder to get Fives to join in on their fun.

Fives are embarrassed by the Seven. Sevens perceive Fives as unresponsive and cold. Sevens become pushy and demanding. Fives become uncooperative and further withdrawn.

This pairing requires an uncritical partner to help them work out their differences. A high level of trust is important to repair this relationship.

5 & 8

Type Five with Type Eight

Overview

Fives and Eights insist on independence. They are aware of boundaries and despise intrusion. Fives and Eights enjoy debate and appreciate someone with strong character. They feel like outcasts and can understand each other on a deeper level. Despite their need for space, Fives and Eight may discover their vulnerabilities and sense of need for their partner. Both types tend to ignore their own unhappiness and suffering.

Fives need to be more in tune with their instinctive energy. They need to engage with the practical world and accept their own sense of power. Eights need to be more aware of the impact their actions have on themselves and their environment. In consideration of their partners, they need to consider consequences before they act.

As a couple, Fives and Eights bring action, thoughtfulness, power, depth, brashness, and brilliance to their relationship. Together, they serve as confidantes for one another, and protect and advise each other.

Potential Trouble

Fives and Eights need to understand and accepts that certain values differ between them. Eights take pride in their worldly achievements and status. Conversely, Fives feel valuable to the world when they can sacrifice their personal luxuries for advancement. Fives are indifferent to the physical and practical goals Eights have.

Eights use their might and energy to intimidate and gain control. Therefore, they can become threatening and confrontational in the relationship. Fives can lose respect for their partner if they perceive them as destructive and irrational. They will physically leave to gain a feeling of security. Eights will retaliate in any way possible. If the Eight leaves first, Fives will react to rejection with cynicism and depression.

Fives and Eights are both sensitive to rejection. Unfortunately, they both experience feelings of rejection easily. Fives shut down in response to stress, making it difficult to work through relationship issues.

5 & 9

Type Five with Type Nine

Overview

Fives and Nines are characterized by respect for each other's individualism. Along with that respect, comes an acknowledgement of boundaries. Not a clingy pair, Fives and Nines offer emotional and personal space to their partner for enjoying separate activities. They don't intrude or hover over their partner, yet they can still have a healthy emotional interest in each other.

Nines are uncritical and undemanding. Despite being the more emotional between the two, Nines do not always know how to express their feelings. Nines appreciate the Five's ability to ask the right questions to pull the right things out of them. Fives appreciate the Nine's warm and nurturing qualities. Nines can help Fives to relax.

Fives and Nines may help open each other's perspectives by introducing alternative worldviews for each other through their relationship.

Potential Trouble

Between the two, Nines are more emotionally available, but both Fives and Nines can be so out of touch with their feelings, they do not even truly know how they feel about each other.

Generally, no one can live up to the fantasy image Nines create around their partner. Nines tend to idealize their partner, especially when they are together. But with the Five absent, Nines can get an "out of sight, out of mind" perspective regarding their significant other. Fives perceive the "out of sight, out of mind" attitude as an on/off relationship. They become frustrated, cynical, and depressed about the union.

Tensions between Fives and Nines grow due to the space they are willing to give each other. They are aware and respectful of boundaries and would not want to intrude on someone's boundaries, but this widening chasm between the two will eventually cause a gap so wide between them, that it is difficult to come back together and connect. Without a substantial effort to see each other frequently, the relationship between Fives and Nines will evaporate away.

Fives and Nines can become disconnected not only from each other, but from themselves. They live in their imagination, rather than reality – especially the Nine. As the relationship starts to deteriorate, solitary interests steal the Five's attention, while the pursuit of peace and more supportive relationships draw away the Nine.

6 & 6

Double Type Sixes

Overview

Strong Six couples make a point to understand each other. Two Sixes usually bond quickly, sensing a kindred spirit. Double Sixes will have shared secrets and values. They stimulate each other intellectually.

Trust is extremely important to Sixes. They can allow themselves to relax and enjoy themselves by developing a deep trust between them. Trust allows double Six couples to voice their doubts and suspicions, to test ideas, and to discover how they really feel about situations. They give each other a lot of mutual support and protection. They will rush to the other's aid without hesitation. Loyalty and commitment reinforce the feelings of safety and security they build together.

There may also be a lot of unspoken sensitivity in a double Six relationship. Sixes are not skillful at talking about their feelings directly. They express their feelings and attitudes through their actions and through their dedication and steadfastness. They inspire each other to work towards happiness – more so than they would for themselves.

Potential Trouble

Sixes can sometimes act on impulse, without thinking through their situation or finding a viable solution to their problems. They may make decisions haphazardly due to their anxiety. Alternatively, double Sixes can freeze and become indecisive and fall into a stalemate and a feeling of confusion, unable to act. They will blame each other for the situation and for not providing a solution. They will continue to shift the blame back and forth to buy time to work through their anxiety until they reach a solution.

Double Six couples tend to be emotionally reactive. For this reason, they can be oversensitive and argumentative with each other. Double Sixes can be a very tense pairing with lots of outbursts, yelling, arguments, and blaming.

Unhealthy Sixes may be semi-hysterical and keep everyone on edge with their nervous pessimism. Double Sixes have fears which are based on speculations about the future and irrational. Therefore, it can be difficult to break the pattern of anxiety between this pair. Once a spirit of negativity creeps in, they begin to feed off each other's fears. Double Sixes can get into worst-case scenarios and other forms of magnifying problems until they both feel like crises are everywhere and believe they are doomed.

Double Sixes tend to wear each other out with their worrying, negativity, suspicion, and eventual mistrust of each other. This type of couple may find it near impossible to reestablish trust due to each other's accusations, feelings of betrayal, and lack of support.

6 & 7

Type Six with Type Seven

Overview

Sixes and Sevens are both intellectual. Together, they can offer reinforcement of each other's strengths. In certain areas, they counterbalance the other person's limitations. Sevens are entertaining and uplifting to Sixes. They are quick witted and enjoy banter with their partner. Sixes bring commitment and loyalty to the Seven.

When it comes to bringing goals to fruition, Sixes and Sevens each provide valuable offerings that bring out the best in their partner, and help each other maximize their personal potential. Sevens are good at calming the fears of Sixes and helping Sixes move beyond those fears. Sevens rely on the expertise and grounded nature of Sixes. Sixes are more in touch with reality and what can be accomplished with the limitations at hand. Sevens are the brainstormers, while Sixes are good at implementing plans to get the job done. Sevens teach Sixes resilience and how not to fear the future while Sixes teach Sevens the difference between optimism and a pipedream.

Potential Trouble

Sixes and Sevens may complement each other's strengths when they are healthy. However, in the average to lower levels, the picture can shift quickly. These two types have opposing viewpoints that reflect different expectations and philosophies for life and relationships. These differences can be too vast to overcome.

The Six's tendency towards pessimism and negativity can wear on the Seven's tendency to be optimistic and positive. Sevens are interested in overcoming limitations, seeing new possibilities, and trying new things. On the opposite side of the spectrum, Sixes live a life of self-imposed rules and limits. They value predictability and security, sometimes causing them to foresee problems and creating plans to prevent future problems that never arise. Sevens feel that Sixes worry too much, making themselves (and those around them) crazy by raising questions and objections about everything before trying anything new. Sixes oppose everything. These differences make it hard for Sevens to feel like they can live their lives to their highest potential alongside their partner.

The Six's desire for security and predictability causes them to want a partner who they can have a long-term commitment with. The Seven thrives off of things being new and fresh in their lives, so they can be more reluctant to enter relationships requiring a long-term commitment. The Seven's thirst for "something new" leads the Six to feel that the Seven is too self-indulgent. Sixes can also fear that this desire for "something new" bleeds over into their relationship. Sixes grow distrustful and get suspicious easily, questioning the loyalty of their Seven partner. As trust deteriorates for the Six, so does the relationship, and as excitement deteriorates for the Seven, so does the relationship.

6 & 8

Type Six with Type Eight

Overview

Sixes and Eights can build an exceptionally strong and long lasting relationship. They believe life is highly unpredictable, therefore, a primary aim for them is to create a safe and secure environment for themselves and their loved ones. Sixes and Eights both admire honesty, loyalty, hard work, responsibility, and courage. Sixes desire connection and commitment. They bring sensitivity, warmth, and playfulness to the relationship.

These two can make a great problem solving pair that will excel at pushing through life's challenges. Sixes are more intellectual. Their skepticism and analytical thinking give them the ability to think through decisions and foresee potential problems before acting. Eights take charge, and provide the leadership and gumption that Sixes can lack.

In fact, challenges and adversity energize Eights and their "can-do" spirit. Sixes admire their Eight partner's strong will and confidence, idealizing the Eight as their hero. Eights are warmed by their partner's devotion and admiration. The Six can soften the Eight's hard exterior.

Both types feel that most people are selfish and can't be trusted, therefore, both have longstanding issues with trust and may put each other through tests to determine the other's loyalty. While fireworks between these types may be inevitable at times, with genuine affection, the bond between them will still grow stronger over time. Once these two have bonded, it is hard to pull them apart, despite any changes that may occur in the relationship.

Potential Trouble

Both types are emotional, but don't always know how to face their emotions. Eights hide their emotions and vulnerability under a facade of toughness and bravado. Sixes hide their emotions and vulnerability under a shell of defensiveness and bluster. Both types will counterattack when they feel threatened, but Eights will become condescending toward Sixes if they feel Sixes are wavering and weak in their position.

Eights set the tone and take leadership in the relationship. They expect others to adapt to them instead of the other way around. Eights are amused by the seeming independence of others because they see themselves as the only one capable of being in charge.

Most of the time, Sixes can handle and appreciate the Eight's leadership. However, there are times when they feel the need to push back and prove they are nobody's puppet. This creates a power struggle within the relationship, which leads to more fights.

An anxious Six will attempt to avoid confrontation with their overbearing Eight partner, leading to passive aggressive behavior. Eights will sense this and question the Six's loyalty. The Eight's tendency towards rage only exacerbates the relationship problems here.

6 & 9

Type Six with Type Nine

Overview

Sixes and Nines can be a very stable relationship. Despite their differences, deep down they desire the same things. Sixes need security and predictability, while Nines need autonomy and stability. Both types need a solid foundation they can depend on. Sixes and Nines use their childhood experiences and beliefs to guide them in adulthood. They seek a partner with similar beliefs and values.

While they experience many similarities, they are still very different. Sixes are more skeptical and questioning of the world around them. Nines offer more optimism and acceptance. Sixes expect their partner to prove themselves to them, while Nines may be too trusting and sometimes naïve. When it comes to banding together to solve problems as a couple, Sixes tend to spot "exceptions" and focus on the complications of a situation, rather than find an acceptable solution. Nines can see the overall picture better and find a solution to fix their problem.

Both types have difficulty defining what makes them special as a person. However, together they can bolster one another's confidence through their harmony with each other. Sixes and Nines with a balanced relationship may believe they have found their soulmate.

Potential Trouble

Communication is a common problem between these two. Trouble comes when they start to clam up and can't express their problems with each other. They want to make the other person guess what's wrong, rather than just communicating. Both types can become defensive and stubborn. Their stubbornness may create a stalemate between the couple.

Sixes and Nines both value familiarity and security, and if they are in lower levels of development, they can fight to protect and uphold those values in very unhealthy ways. Nines will meddle and manipulate to keep the relationship together. In extreme cases, they may take advantage of physical or even psychological health problems to guilt their partner into taking care of them. Sixes frequently feel guilty and do whatever they can to make up and keep their position secure.

Avoiding confrontation is all too common between these types. Sixes tend to have the shorter fuse and may explode on the Nine, creating sometimes irreparable damage to the relationship.

7 & 7

Double Type Sevens

Overview

Sevens represent spontaneity, high energy, and interest in anything fresh and exciting. When Sevens are well balanced and healthy, there is a sense of abundance and joy that permeates their relationship and overflows to those around them. Healthy Sevens will exude happiness.

Sevens are sensitive, generous, thoughtful, and idealistic. They are sociable and provide good company for each other. They expect personal freedom and don't want to be tied down by commitments or routine. They are careful not to impose too many rules or expectations on each other.

Sevens are resilient and optimistic. They are ready to start over with a fresh perspective when they encounter difficulties. Their relationship is guided by their gratitude for having each other.

Potential Trouble

Despite their positive commonalities, Sevens lack the patience needed to develop a relationship with a truly solid foundation. They want a complete, mature, fully developed relationship right away without pressing through the things that relationships have to go through in order to get to that level. Their high expectations make it difficult to work through the growing pains of a relationship.

Sevens may seek other endeavors when the relationship is no longer stimulating and exciting. Sevens hate commitment because they always feel like they are missing out on something better. Another issue that can arise in double Seven relationships is that neither person wants to be the first to risk commitment and rejection even if they have strong feelings for their partner.

Sevens are often impulsive and don't consider the consequences of their actions and words. They act in the heat of the moment. They tend to be insensitive towards each other in these moments.

Sevens crave constant stimulation socially. This is great if their social lives mesh, but takes a toll on the relationship when they don't. They lose interest in spending time together, and each person is determined not to get rejected by the other.

7 & 8

Type Seven with Type Eight

Overview

Sevens and Eights are independent, strong-willed, and assertive. Both types are outspoken in their opinions and their needs. They resist being controlled by authority or their partner. They often respond with defiance, and push the limits.

Both types are prone to overspending because they want to impress others with their money and flaunt it as a symbol of their success. A good financial plan is essential to prevent financial strain in a Type Seven, Type Eight relationship.

When it comes to energy, boldness, and zeal for life, this is an excellent pairing. Both types are active, with exceptional vitality. They love to try new things and have a strong sense of adventure. Extreme sports, even intramural sports, and "out of the box" travel make for excellent bonding opportunities for this couple.

Sevens keep their communication light and fun. They are highly engaging storytellers and conversationalists. They turn both their troubles and adventures into entertaining tales. Eights can be more reserved and moody, and sometimes need the help of Sevens to lighten their mood and uplift their spirits. Eights bring directness and face difficulties with persistence and determination, making the Eight an ideal partner for "when the going gets tough."

Potential Trouble

Sevens and Eights need to find positive channels for their unique energy and interests. Failure to do so will result in destructive ways of releasing energy, and may cause them to turn against each other.

The strong-willed and independent nature of Sevens and Eights can do more harm than good. Both types can flaunt their defiance as a badge of honor. Unhealthy Eights will bully and threaten Sevens when they don't get what they want. Sevens may become condescending and insulting towards Eights. They can be extremely self-centered, believing that the world must revolve around them and their desires.

Both types are addicted to the adrenaline rush of reckless behavior. Sevens and Eights may verbally abuse their partner with words other people would never even allow themselves to think, much less verbalize. At the most extreme low levels of development, fights between Sevens and Eights can turn into public scenes of verbal and physical violence.

7 & 9

<u>Type Seven with Type Nine</u>

Overview

Seven and Nine partnerships bring a good mix of similar and opposite qualities. Sevens and Nines are both optimistic, upbeat and strive to avoid conflict and negativity. Both types are sociable, friendly, and overall happy with themselves and their lives. They tend to move forward rather than dwell on problems of the past. This leads them to forgive and forget quickly.

Sevens and Nines tend to be practical, but use romance and physical intimacy to spice up their relationship. They use humor to get through the mundane moments of life.

Sevens can stimulate Nines when others can't. Sevens tend to be more assertive than Nines. The Sevens take initiative, bring energy, and lay out plans for the relationship. They are confident, curious, fun, adventurous, and open to new experiences. They are resilient in times of setback.

Nines are steadfast and supportive partners. They provide acceptance and tend to be more sympathetic and soft-hearted. Nines are more relaxed and less demanding than Sevens. They are generous and more willing to make sacrifices to keep their partner happy. There can be a good balance between energy and relaxation between this pair.

Potential Trouble

Sevens and Nines can have difficulty truly working through the rough patches of life and relationships. Due to their relentless optimism, both prefer keeping everything positive and remaining agreeable. However, when problems are brought to light, Sevens are more inclined to talk about those issues. At lower levels of development, Sevens can become verbally abusive toward the Nine.

Sevens feel Nines are indecisive and incompetent. Their criticism and contempt pushes Nines into withdrawal. Sevens justify their criticism by saying honesty mandates that they express their disdain toward the Nine. The Seven's assertiveness can become too much, and their demanding way of being can send Nines into further withdrawal and inaction. They become stubborn and shut down.

What has the potential to be one of the most carefree couple pairings can become miserably strained if the two are unable to communicate their feelings and work out their problems. Making matters worse, when problems arise, neither one is willing to take responsibility for the fall of the relationship.

8 & 8

Double Type Eights

Overview

Few relationships will compare to the intensity between two Eights. Type Eights bring a lot of passion, vitality, and energy. They have strong wills and are independent thinkers. Eights are quick to act on their impulses. They don't just talk about doing something, they go do it. This can add excitement to their relationship.

Two Eights know what it takes to become a team and get things done for the household while creating an environment of security and stability. These two feel confidence in the face of problems that may arise. Their relief to have found someone they believe is as strong and confident as themselves leads to mutual respect. In healthy levels of development, they communicate directly and settle disagreements quickly.

When their levels of development and dominant traits are well matched, double Eights provide unshakable support for one another, and together can build an empire.

Potential Trouble

On the flip side, Double Eights are extremely volatile. Due to the typical characteristics of Type Eights, this can be one of the most explosive pairings. Physical rough-play and verbal assaults can get out of hand because Eights refuse to back down from a conflict and are reluctant to apologize.

They put their partner through frequent tests to earn complete control of the relationship. The power struggle to be in control will be the center of most conflicts. They become competitors and rivals with each other. Unhealthy Eights refuse to back down or "be weak." Eights don't feel satisfied without power in at least one area. They'll badger their partner for power until one person finally taps out. They will need to learn to negotiate, or the relationship will eventually wear down.

Eights have short tempers, and at times suspiciousness and paranoia may start setting in. Eights can need a lot of space, which can push their partner away. They will present tests of loyalty, upping the ante emotionally after each test. Despite their hard exterior, Eights get hurt emotionally very easily and will banish people from their lives over seemingly trivial matters.

8 & 9

Type Eight with Type Nine

Overview

A relationship between Eights and Nines can seem like fire and water. Type Eights have a take-charge attitude other people look up to. They are full of vitality and self-confidence. Nines admire the leadership qualities of their Eight partners, and may try to live vicariously through the Eight's positive traits. Nines are awed by the Eight's fearlessness and ability to make things happen. Eights enjoy having someone who appreciates their brash leadership.

Despite the appearance of having everything under their control, Eights spend a lot of time overcoming hidden demons. They feel they have to "fight to survive" and leave their mark on the world. Nines provide a safe harbor for Eights to relax and let their guard down. Nines bring a sense of stability and calmness that Eights find comforting and necessary for their well-being.

Therefore, they tend to teach each other what the other is lacking. Eights teach Nines self-assertion and confidence. Nines attempt to teach Eights when to fight for their values and when to back down and let go.

Both types have strong willpower. They both enjoy simplicity and comfort. Creating a safe retreat from the world is a common goal. When their goals align, this type of pairing can be powerful, yet comforting at the same time.

Potential Trouble

In some cases, Eights can eventually lose interest in the relationship, feeling that Nines are coming between them and "their plans." When drifting apart, Eights may try to reconnect by trying to find something exciting to do with their partner, but the Nine will typically respond with a "Why bother?" attitude, causing the Eight to feel rejected and undermined.

In other relationships, Nines perceive unhealthy Eights as too bossy and controlling. Nines think Eights are too selfish and want everything their way. Nines may think they want someone with a take-charge attitude, but when that attitude is turned against them, they rebel and become stubborn. Eights think the calmness of Nines presents them as a blank slate that Eights can mold to their needs. However, Eights are not aware of how stubborn Nines can be.

When Eights and Nines are in unhealthy levels of development, their defenses become opposing forces. Eights push harder, and Nines shut down and become unresponsive, pushing their partner away. In response, the Eight's aggression grows, which can lead them to become belligerent. Nines respond by going on strike emotionally.

Rage can become the center of the relationship, deteriorating it into a battlefield with frequent verbal or physical abuse. Eights will start belittling and threatening the Nine. Nines may feel they must protect children or other people they feel would be vulnerable to the Eight's violence and hardness.

9 & 9

Double Type Nines

Overview

As with all double-type relationships, their levels of development, wings, and their unique dominant strengths will determine the success or failure of this relationship. A Double Nines relationship is more common to happen naturally than other same-type relationships.

Supportive, gentle, comfortable, and hospitable are just a few of the words that describe how Nines are with each other. Nines typically seem to have unlimited patience and be quick to forgive. They give each other plenty of affection and attention, however, they know when to give each other space when necessary.

Nines do typically prefer routine and familiarity. They will attempt to create a safe haven to protect and prepare their family for life's ups and downs. However, when trouble does come, Nines are steadfast and do not let troubles become a roadblock in their life or in their relationship. Instead, they look for the positive in the circumstance they are facing. Despite the fact that Nines are easy-going, they will take whatever means necessary to protect their family.

Double Nines typically feel comfortable and unpressured within their relationship Both partners prefer to take life at their own pace. Mellowness is a tell-tale quality of this type of relationship. This carefree environment is one of the main attractions of this type of relationship.

Potential Trouble

The regularity and steadiness Nines prefer can be a double-edged sword for this type of relationship. They fear anything that would intrude or disturb their peace and harmony. When it comes to upholding that truth for factors outside the relationship for instance, Nines will neglect anyone they feel may be a threat to their union, even if it's a close friend or family member who may not agree with their choice of partner for instance.

Double Nines may also get so caught up in creating harmony in their life and relationship, that they are reluctant to bring up important issues. Despite their love for each other, real communication rarely happens. Many times, they keep their frustrations in their head.

Nines in lower levels of development may idealize their partner and relationship. They don't see their partner for who they really are. Most of their perception of the relationship only happens in their imagination. They may not express their concerns with their partner, a habit of which will eventually threaten the relationship. Their quietness in their relationship ultimately leads to built-up tension and resentment. Worry, anxiety, blaming their partner, and passive aggressive behavior will undermine their relationship unless they have an outlet to vent.

On the surface, Double Nines may seem to be a perfect match and have an uncanny ability to get along with each other. However, they may be suppressive of each other. Their suppressive-ness may kill their vitality and ambition and become characterized by depression with seemingly no cause.

They can seem to be amiable and happy, but they may really be stuck in boredom. Yet Double Nines may choose to find a way to coexist with little joy or excitement just to keep the relationship alive.

Sharing is caring.

Let other people know that

you like this book and they will too

by **leaving a review on Amazon!**

Chapter 6:

Putting The Information To Work

Here is a list of 50 key questions to open communication between you and your partner. Based on the information you've learned, this list is designed to help you discuss your enneatypes, pinpoint strengths and weaknesses in yourselves and your relationship, identify "blind spots," and figure out ways to better yourselves and better solve conflict. These questions dig deeper by asking what traits you wish you had and what traits you wish you could avoid. Additionally, you can ask yourselves how to achieve the traits you wish you had.

These questions will help you gain a deeper understanding of your partner, and will ultimately enrich your union. By listening to your partner, you will learn who your partner is, and who they want to be, despite their current actions. Use this information to learn about your partner without judgment, and help each other reach healthier, more stable levels of development.

Many times, it takes the help of other people to become who we truly want to be. Relationships can be a powerful tool for doing just that and maximizing our potential personally, professionally, physically, and spiritually.

Questions

1. What Enneagram type are you?
2. If you could choose a new Enneagram type for yourself, what would you choose?
3. What traits do you value or wish you had?
4. What traits are you most ashamed of?
5. What wing type do you identify with the most?
6. What traits from your stress point do you identify with?
7. What traits from your security point do you identify with?
8. Do you think the Enneagram type descriptions are accurate? Why/Why not?
9. What surprises you about your enneatype?
10. What level(s) of development do you identify with?
11. What is the highest level of development you have reached?
12. What is the lowest level of development you have experienced?
13. What challenges do you struggle with most?
14. How did you overcome your lowest point?
15. How can I help you grow to a higher level of development?
16. What causes stress in your life?
17. What other Enneagram types do you identify with?

18. Do you think your Enneagram type has changed throughout your life?
19. What Enneagram type do you think I am? Why?
20. What traits do you see in me that I may not recognize?
21. What are your favorite traits that you see in me?
22. What surprises you about my enneatype?
23. How do you think our types have influenced our relationship?
24. Do you think the section Type X with Type X accurately describes our relationship?
25. What can we do to avoid the "Potential Trouble" in that section for our relationship?
26. How can we use what we have learned to improve our relationship?
27. What Enneagram type do you think your parents could be?
28. How do you think your parents' types affected how they raised you?
29. How has your childhood affected your Enneagram type?
30. What Enneagram types do you recognize in people around you?
31. How have they influenced you?
32. Do you think you can influence your type by hanging out with certain people?
33. What do you feel has had the most impact on who you are and the choices you make? (DNA, how you were raised, social influence, media influence, personal choice, etc)

34. What effect did your Enneagram type have on our last conflict?
35. What can we do differently next time?
36. What have you learned about your Enneagram type? (As it relates to conflict)
37. What have you learned about my Enneagram type? (As it relates to conflict)
38. What are some additional insights you can teach me about your Enneagram type?
39. How does your Enneagram type affect the decisions you make?
40. Describe what it is like being Type X?
41. What have you learned about yourself?
42. What have you learned about me?
43. Do the Enneagram type descriptions help you understand why I sometimes act the way I do?
44. Do you think you will understand others better now that you have learned about the Enneagram types?
45. Do you feel in control of your choices?
46. How can you gain control of the choices you make?
47. Do you think your understanding of the Enneagram will help you make different choices?
48. Were you familiar with the Enneagram before reading this book?
49. What were you hoping to learn from this book?
50. What do you feel is the most important thing you have learned from this book?

Conclusion

Congratulations! By now, you should have an understanding of the Enneagram, your enneatype, your partner's enneatype, and your relationship dynamics. Hopefully, you can see and understand why you both react the way you do in different situations, and see what to strive for in your relationship and what to look out for and avoid. This should help you in achieving your goals of self-discovery and reconciling differences in your relationship.

But don't stop here. Don't just consume this information—take action and put it to use. Be sure to actually use the discussion questions in the last chapter to go deeper with your partner. And revisit those questions as needed over the course of your relationship. These are great questions to use as journal prompts, but they are most effective when using them to guide direct, face to face conversation with your partner.

Thank you again for choosing this book. Every effort was made to ensure that it is full of as much useful information as possible.

Finally, if you have found this book informative or helpful in any way, please leave a review on Amazon.

And be on the lookout for more books and audiobooks by Steven Miles on Amazon.com and Audible.com.

Thank you!

And good luck on your journey to mastering yourself and your relationship.

Made in the USA
Monee, IL
03 January 2020